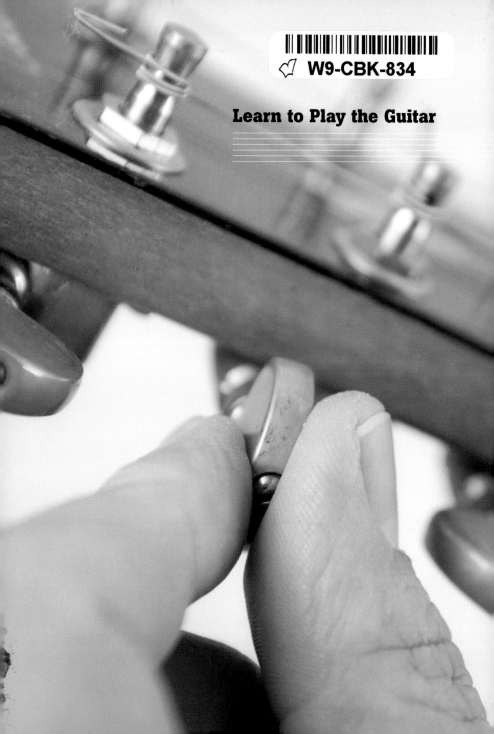

Learn to Play the Guitar

Learn to Play the Guitar

A beginner's guide to playing acoustic and electric guitar

Phil Capone

CHARTWELL
BOOKS, INC.

Contents

A QUARTO BOOK

Published in 2007 by
CHARTWELL BOOKS, INC.
A division of BOOK SALES, INC.
276 Fifth Avenue Suite 206
New York, New York 10001
USA
Reprinted 2007, 2008, 2009
Copyright © 2007 Quarto Inc.

ISBN-13: 978-0-7858-2189-2
ISBN-10: 0-7858-2189-9
QUAR.LPG

This book was designed
and produced by
Quarto Publishing plc
The Old Brewery
6 Blundell Street
London N7 9BH

Project Editor Mary Groom
Art Editor and Designer
  Tania Field
Photographer Martin Norris
Proofreader Nicholas Barnett
Indexer Diana LeCore
Assistant Art Director
  Penny Cobb

Art Director Moira Clinch
Publisher Paul Carslake

Manufactured by Modern Age
  Repro House Ltd, Hong Kong
Printed by 1010 Printing
  International Limited, China

Chord library   148

Scale library   176

Buyer's guide   226

Introduction

There is a bewildering choice of "teach yourself" guitar books on the market today. What sets this book apart from the rest is that it has been designed to get you playing with the minimum of fuss. As well as conventional TAB, easy rhythmic notation is also provided. Too many self-tutor guitar books gloss over this crucial element, leaving the student confused, frustrated, and unable to get the music off the page and onto their guitar. By using the rhythmic notation in conjunction with the accompanying CD, you will be left in no doubt how each piece should sound and how to play it correctly.

A dogmatic approach to technique has been avoided throughout—the ideal hand positions and best posture are indicated early in the book to help you to avoid developing frustrating bad habits. This is no manual for either the electric guitarist or the acoustic guitarist either; it is intended as a "bible" for the budding guitarist. The professional guitarist is expected to be equally proficient on both electric and acoustic guitar. While this book can't promise to turn you into a pro, it will provide you with the necessary techniques for playing electric and acoustic styles, clearly explaining how to use both pick and fingerstyle techniques throughout. You don't need to own two guitars to get the most out of this book either—each lesson has been designed to work on just about any kind of guitar.

Not only does this book provide you with over thirty self-contained lessons (many teaching you the tune and accompaniment), it also provides you with an essential chord library containing two chord shapes for every major, minor, and dominant seventh chord you will ever need. A scale resource clearly illustrates two different positions for four essential scale types in all twelve keys. Finally, an unbiased and extensive buyer's guide explains not just the different types of guitars available, but also which amplifier is best for you and what essential accessories you may need.

Finally, the handy and compact spiral-bound layout makes it easy to carry this book around with you. Because it opens out flat it's guaranteed to make learning a pleasure. So grab your guitar and let's get started!

About the chord and scale libraries

To help you get the most out of the chord and scale libraries, you should read through the following glossary of icons and symbols. Theory and "music speak" has been kept to a minimum so that you can get shapes off the page and onto your guitar as quickly as possible. So now all you have to do is get playing and start having fun!

Chord library

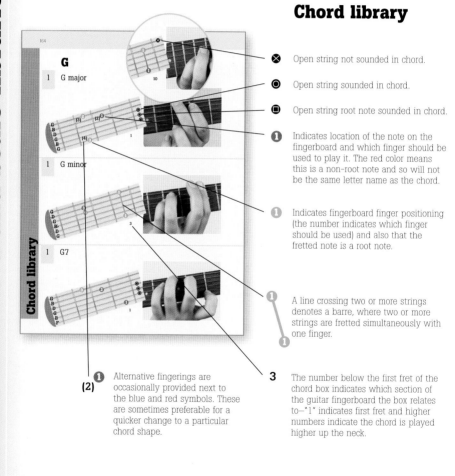

Open string not sounded in chord.

Open string sounded in chord.

Open string root note sounded in chord.

Indicates location of the note on the fingerboard and which finger should be used to play it. The red color means this is a non-root note and so will not be the same letter name as the chord.

Indicates fingerboard finger positioning (the number indicates which finger should be used) and also that the fretted note is a root note.

A line crossing two or more strings denotes a barre, where two or more strings are fretted simultaneously with one finger.

(2) Alternative fingerings are occasionally provided next to the blue and red symbols. These are sometimes preferable for a quicker change to a particular chord shape.

3 The number below the first fret of the chord box indicates which section of the guitar fingerboard the box relates to—"1" indicates first fret and higher numbers indicate the chord is played higher up the neck.

Scale library

There are five possible shapes for every scale on the guitar which, when joined end-to-end, cover the fingerboard in the notes of one specific scale. However, rather than overwhelm you with too much information, only the two most important shapes are given for each scale: Shape 1 (which is formed from the open E chord and associated six-string barre chord), and Shape 4 (formed from the open A shape and associated five-string barre chord).

Scale fingerings are kept to a minimum to keep the diagram as clear as possible. Don't forget that scales should be played strictly "in position"—so if you look at the C major scale Shape 1 on page 178, you will notice that only the lower fingerings are annotated. This is because the scale is played entirely in seventh position, i.e. with the first finger on the seventh fret. The second finger will then fret the notes on the eighth fret; the third finger the notes on the ninth, and so on. Additional fingerings indicate an "out of position" stretch or a position shift up or down part way through the scale—for example, Shape 4 of the C major scale on the same page shifts from second position to third position for the highest five notes.

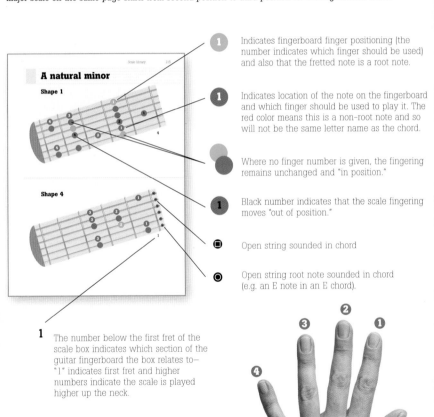

1️⃣ Indicates fingerboard finger positioning (the number indicates which finger should be used) and also that the fretted note is a root note.

1️⃣ Indicates location of the note on the fingerboard and which finger should be used to play it. The red color means this is a non-root note and so will not be the same letter name as the chord.

⚪ Where no finger number is given, the fingering remains unchanged and "in position."

1 Black number indicates that the scale fingering moves "out of position."

⬛ Open string sounded in chord

◎ Open string root note sounded in chord (e.g. an E note in an E chord).

A natural minor

Shape 1

Shape 4

1 The number below the first fret of the scale box indicates which section of the guitar fingerboard the box relates to— "1" indicates first fret and higher numbers indicate the scale is played higher up the neck.

Finger numbers
Standard hand fingering has been used throughout.

The fingerboard

Finding notes on the fingerboard is not easy; even accomplished players can be sketchy on this knowledge if they have learnt primarily "by ear." This easy-to-use diagram is intended to help you locate any note on the fingerboard—fast! Remember that after the twelfth fret the entire fingerboard repeats an octave higher (starting with the open string note name).

Fingerboard repetition

12th fret is the same as open strings then note name repeats, e.g. fret 13 is the same as fret 1.

Fret 1

6 – **F**
5 – **A#/Bb**
4 – **D#/Eb**
3 – **G#/Ab**
2 – **C**
1 – **F**

Fret 2

6 – **F#/Gb**
5 – **B**
4 – **E**
3 – **A**
2 – **C#/Db**
1 – **F#/Gb**

Fret 3

6 – **G**
5 – **C**
4 – **F**
3 – **A#/Bb**
2 – **D**
1 – **G**

Fret 4

6 – **G#/Ab**
5 – **C#/Db**
4 – **F#/Gb**
3 – **B**
2 – **D#/Eb**
1 – **G#/Ab**

Fret 5

6 – **A**
5 – **D**
4 – **G**
3 – **C**
2 – **E**
1 – **A**

Fret 6

6 – **A#/Bb**
5 – **D#/Eb**
4 – **G#/Ab**
3 – **C#/Db**
2 – **F**
1 – **A#/Bb**

Fret 7

6 – **B**
5 – **E**
4 – **A**
3 – **D**
2 – **F#/Gb**
1 – **B**

Fret 8

6 – **C**
5 – **F**
4 – **A#/Bb**
3 – **D#/Eb**
2 – **G**
1 – **C**

Fret 9

6 – **C#/Db**
5 – **F#/Gb**
4 – **B**
3 – **E**
2 – **G#/Ab**
1 – **C#/Db**

Fret 10

6 – **D**
5 – **G**
4 – **C**
3 – **F**
2 – **A**
1 – **D**

Fret 11

6 – **D#/Eb**
5 – **G#/Ab**
4 – **C#/Db**
3 – **F#/Gb**
2 – **A#/Bb**
1 – **D#/Eb**

Fret 12

6 – **E**
5 – **A**
4 – **D**
3 – **G**
2 – **B**
1 – **E**

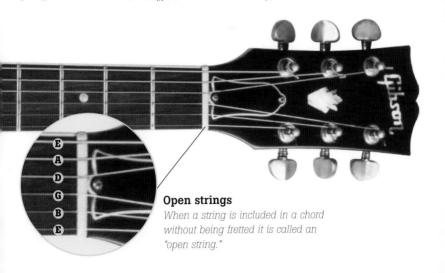

Open strings

When a string is included in a chord without being fretted it is called an "open string."

Notes for left-handed players

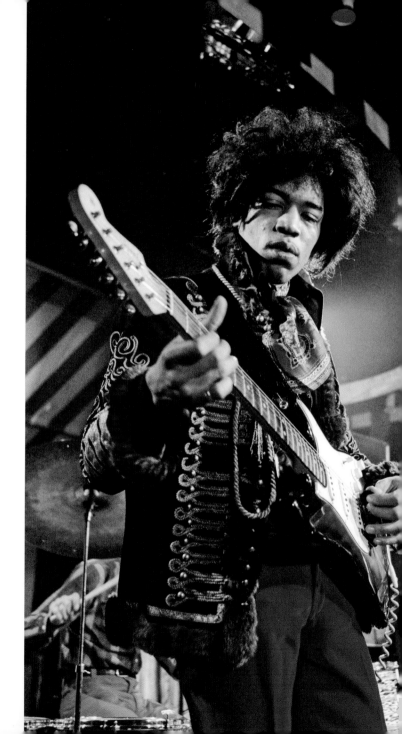

Notes for left-handed players

The left-handed guitarist has an additional dilemma to face. Is it best to buy a left-handed instrument from the start, or simply to learn to play right-handed and enjoy the wider choice of instruments available to "righties?" Because the fretting hand is very important (and this is actually the right hand of a left-handed player), many left-handed folk simply opt to play a right-handed guitar. After all, there is no such thing as a left-handed piano, so would it be such a bad thing to play a guitar right-handed from the word go? Only you can really answer that question. However, you should certainly try out a few left-handed and right-handed guitars in a music store before you make your decision. Don't worry if you can't play anything yet; just sit down with the instrument and pick a couple of open strings. If a left-handed instrument feels more natural to hold, then you should follow your instinct.

Adapting a right-handed guitar

Jimi Hendrix immortalized the image of a right-handed guitar turned upside-down and re-strung, but this can cause a wealth of intonation and tuning problems. The cut-away of an electric guitar will also be on the wrong side of the neck, making access to high notes more difficult.

There are also some players (usually self-taught) who learn to play a right-handed guitar turned upside down and not re-strung! This means that the high E string would be closest to you and everything would, in effect, be back to front. And all of your chord shapes would have to be played upside down—a potential nightmare! Although this is the least recommended option for left-handed players, it serves to illustrate that there are no hard and fast rules.

In the long run, it can be a lot less hassle to simply buy a left-handed guitar; all of the key components (i.e. the bridge, nut, body, and neck) are already reversed to ensure that instrument is comfortable to play and will remain in tune.

Using this book

As far as reading music goes, TAB follows the conventions of standard notation (i.e. the pitches on the stave don't relate to the guitar visually), so whether you play left- or right-handed shouldn't matter. Chord and scale boxes are a little trickier since the shape or pattern has to be reversed. However, this is not as complicated as it sounds, and many "lefties" can decipher them instantly with a little practice. There are, of course, also many excellent scale and chord books written exclusively for left-handed players should you find this process too confusing.

Left-handed guitar
This is a left-handed Gibson 335. The volume and tone controls, pick-up selector, scratchplate, and bridge have all been repositioned.

Famous left-handed player

The legendary Jimi Hendrix playing a "reverse strung" right-handed Fender Stratocaster upside down.

Lessons

Lesson 1
Getting in tune

There's nothing more off-putting than playing an out-of-tune guitar, so make sure you know how to tune your instrument properly from the start. It's surprising how many guitarists don't think tuning is important, and this isn't just a beginner's issue. The story is often told about the guitarist (usually anonymous) at an audition, who is accomplished and ready to show off their musical skills, but who hears the word "next!" after playing a few bars—a career opportunity missed because they hadn't tuned up properly. So remember, if your guitar is not in tune, it won't sound good. Try to make tuning as instinctive as putting on your seatbelt in the car—each time you pick up your guitar, check the tuning.

Using your ear

This method is called "relative tuning" as it is used to check that the guitar is in tune with itself. Using the TAB as a guide (see Lesson 5 on page 24), you will be able to check each string, starting with the lowest. The notes should be sounded simultaneously for the best results. When the pitches are close, you will hear a beating or pulsating effect caused by the difference in pitch; as the pitches get closer, the beating slows and should disappear altogether when the strings are in tune.

Using a tuner

Electronic tuners are usually automatic. This doesn't mean that they tune the guitar for you, simply that they can recognize which string is being played so you don't have to fiddle around with any switches. The tuner will indicate with an LED arrow and/or dial reading how sharp or flat the string is. All you then have to do is adjust the appropriate tuning peg. Unfortunately, if your guitar is completely out of tune, the tuner won't be able to identify the pitch of the string correctly, so don't be afraid to ask your local music store (or a guitar-playing friend) to help you retune if this happens.

Relative tuning

Tune the strings in pairs as indicated (both notes should sound the same). It doesn't matter which finger you use to fret the notes as long as you don't touch the string above—you need to hear both strings ringing simultaneously.

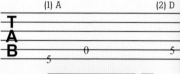

Checking the sixth and fifth strings.

Which way do I turn the pegs?

Once you've discovered an out-of-tune string, the next problem is how to get it back in tune. The guitar's tuners are located on the headstock, either as six along the top or three on each side, depending on which model you have (on acoustics, these are called machine heads or tuning pegs). Identify which peg belongs to the string you want to adjust (this will soon become second nature) and turn it anticlockwise to sharpen the pitch or clockwise to flatten it. If you're not sure which way is which, play the note as you turn it so you can hear the note change; don't move it too far in one go, though—just a fraction of a turn is usually all that is needed.

Lessons

Top tip

When plugging into an electronic tuner, make sure that the volume is turned up full. If you're tuning an acoustic (with the tuner's built-in mic), rest the tuner on your leg as close to the soundhole as possible.

On the CD: track 1

To help you get in tune more easily, follow the tuning notes on the accompanying CD—each string is played three times.

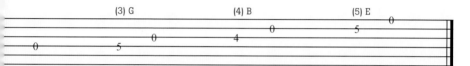

Checking the fifth and fourth strings.

Checking the fourth and third strings.

Checking the third and second strings (at the fourth fret).

Checking the second and first strings.

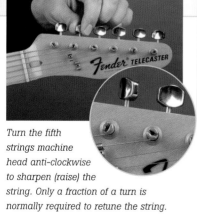

Turn the fifth strings machine head anti-clockwise to sharpen (raise) the string. Only a fraction of a turn is normally required to retune the string.

Turn the machine head clockwise to sharpen the string when adjusting the "G," "B," or "E" strings on a guitar with opposing machine heads

Lesson 2
Are you sitting comfortably?

Correct posture is very important; bad posture can cause muscular problems, so this is a serious matter. Almost all guitarists practice from a sitting position; screwing up your face in mock pain while wielding a low-slung six-string may look cool, but it won't impress anyone if you can't play a note! Remember that it's important to be comfortable when you're practicing and you should also try to avoid unnecessary muscle fatigue. Think of the following advice as a guide for achieving good posture rather than the threat "you'll never learn if you don't sit exactly like this."

Many electric guitar players like to use a strap when practicing with a solid-bodied instrument. This not only raises the height of the guitar so you're not hunched over it, but it also helps to spread your weight so the blood supply is not cut off to one of your legs (the resulting "pins and needles" are painful).

Top tip

Practicing with the guitar at an awkward angle makes playing more difficult and consequently your progress is slower.

Lean back slightly, resting against the back of the chair if there is one.

Place the guitar with the curved, indented underside of the body over your right thigh.

Lessons

The thickest string (low E) should be nearest to you and the thinnest string (high E) should be closest to the floor.

The guitar neck should be roughly parallel with the floor.

Legs should be uncrossed.

Headstock pointing to the left.

When sitting correctly, the back of the guitar should be in contact with your stomach.

Lesson 3
The right-hand position

The problem with teaching any contemporary guitar style is that there is no right or wrong way to play. Classical guitar music has been played for so long that it has evolved its own set of rules; contemporary guitar styles, however, are still in their infancy and many of the music's pioneers were completely self-taught. It is often their unorthodox approach to the instrument that makes them unique. Unfortunately, many teachers are dogmatic about picking technique. This is wrong, because while they may have discovered a system that works for themselves, it won't necessarily work for you. Why spend ages developing the optimum shred-metal picking technique, when all you want to do is play the blues? Contemporary guitar playing is all about individuality; it's about creating your own sound. What if Wes Montgomery had been discouraged from playing with his thumb, or Eddie Van Halen was told not to "tap" on the fingerboard? The following right-hand positions are intended to provide versatile, nongenre specific techniques that will allow your playing skills to grow unhindered by bad habits.

Holding the pick

Grasp the pick between your thumb and first finger. Notice how little of the pick remains visible and how it protrudes at a right angle to the thumb—the more of the pick you hold, the easier it is to control.

Top tip

Don't be afraid to experiment with different types and thicknesses of pick— you may find some more comfortable than others. For fingerstyle playing, try using a thumb pick

Right-hand position using a pick

Try "anchoring" the picking hand by gently resting your third and fourth fingers on the scratchplate (these should be loosely held in position so they are free to move as you pick across the strings).

Right-hand position for fingerpicking

When fingerpicking, your hand should be suspended above the strings with your thumb remaining parallel to the bass strings. If you keep your fingers in a "clawlike" shape, you will be able to pick the strings without moving your hand.

Lesson 4
The left-hand position

Since your left hand does most of the hard work when you're playing, it's important to develop a smooth technique that will allow you to fret notes with the minimum of effort and maximum economy of movement. Contemporary guitarists can learn a lot from their classically trained cousins whose art form has evolved over a long period. The left-hand technique of classical guitarists has been perfected over hundreds of years. One thing is certain—if you don't make a conscious effort to develop a good left-hand technique, you'll join the thousands of guitarists who have had to relearn this technique in order to reach the next level. A professional guitarist can make playing look easy and effortless; this is not because they have a special gift, but because they have spent years perfecting their technique.

Left-hand thumb position
It's important to keep your thumb behind the guitar neck; some players will occasionally use their thumb to fret notes on the sixth string, but keeping it in this position permanently will put unnecessary strain on your fretting hand.

Lessons

Top tip

Try to keep your left-hand thumb pointing upward at the back of the guitar neck and your fingers hovering over the strings.

Angling your fingers

Make sure the tip of each finger approaches the fretboard directly from above and at a 90-degree angle (to avoid damping adjacent strings). It's also important to fret the note close to the fret to avoid weak and buzzy notes.

Keeping close to the fretboard

By keeping your fingers hovering above the strings, you will be able to fret notes more easily as less finger movement will be required (you will find it hard to do this with your little finger at first).

Lesson 5
Reading the TAB

Finding the notes

TAB is short for "tablature," a simplified system of notation widely used for the guitar. The history of TAB dates back to the Renaissance period (1400–1600) when it was used to notate lute music. Today, it can be found in guitar publications all over the world—there are even websites devoted to TAB.

The first example shows six lines forming a system of music known as a stave. The six lines represent the six strings of the guitar, starting with the lowest, E, at the bottom. To read the TAB, all you have to do is translate the numbers to frets on the correct string.

In Example 1 the first two notes are the open (0) sixth string (E), followed by the third fret (3) on the sixth string (G)—it's as easy as that! Simultaneous notes are simply "stacked" as shown at the end of Example 1, where you would play the open (0) third string (G) and open (0) fourth string (D) together (this is called a double stop).

Rhythm

TAB, like anything that has been simplified, has its limitations; the lack of rhythm and fingering indication makes it a sketchy guide at best. To remedy this problem, a conventional stave of music is often added above the TAB. Rather than confuse the issue with too much information, only rhythmic notation has been used (photos will be used to show fingering). This kind of notation is frequently used in contemporary music where guitar parts often containing nothing more than chord symbols are written above a rhythm. The "notes" are characters adapted from standard notation, the difference being the shape of the notehead (conventional "hollow" notes become diamond shapes, while "solid" notes become a slash), and how it is placed on the stave (it fills the middle two spaces). Example 4 is simply Example 1 with the rhythm added above.

Pick direction

Alternate strumming shares the same symbols as alternate picking.

 down pick

 up pick

Example 1

Example 2

Note: If a note has a dot placed beside it the value is increased by half, i.e. a dotted half note becomes three beats long.

Example 3

Note: If a rest has a dot placed beside it the value is increased by half, i.e. a dotted half rest becomes three beats long.

Example 4

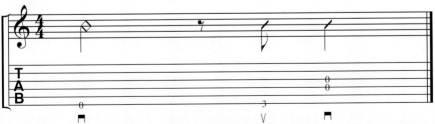

Lesson 6
Getting started: three easy chord shapes

Incredible as it may sound, when you've mastered the "three-chord trick" you will be able to impress your friends by playing a sequence of just three simple chords to literally hundreds of songs. Without getting too involved in theory, each major key contains three chords that form the basis of the three-chord trick: the I or tonic chord, the IV or subdominant chord, and the V or dominant chord. In the key of G, these are the chords of G (I), C (IV), and D (V). Chords I, IV, and V are often referred to as the "primary chords" in any key. Once you've mastered these shapes, the next step is to learn how to change quickly between them. Take a moment to think about how far each finger needs to move, which finger has to move the furthest, etc. You will find that thinking the movement through before you play will really help you to progress.

Famous three-chord songs

The following is a short list of some classic songs that can be played using the three-chord trick (these songs were originally recorded in various keys):

- *Blue Suede Shoes*
  Elvis Presley
- *Johnny B Goode*
  Chuck Berry
- *Bye Bye Love*
  The Everly Brothers
- *Wild Thing*
  The Troggs/Jimi Hendrix
- *Peaceful Easy Feeling*
  The Eagles
- *Sweet Home Alabama*
  Lynyrd Skynyrd
- *Rock & Roll*
  Led Zeppelin
- *Love Me Do*
  The Beatles
- *La Bamba*
  Richie Valens
- *Lay Down Sally*
  Eric Clapton
- *Big Yellow Taxi*
  Joni Mitchell
- *Blowin' in the Wind*
  Bob Dylan

Chord spelling

The term "major" is not usually included in the chord symbol (unlike minor or seventh chords, for instance). So C major is simply written as "C" and G major as "G."

Max up your practice

When you're practicing, try visualizing what you're going to play beforehand. This will help you to be really clear about what you want your fingers to do before you pick up your guitar.

G

This chord has a big stretch between the second and third fingers. You may find this tricky at first, so be patient!

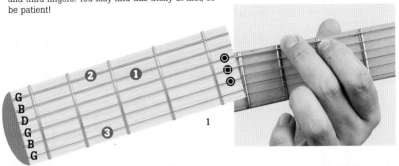

C

Check each note individually to make sure you're not damping the open strings in this chord. Try adjusting the angle of your fingers if there are any "dead" notes.

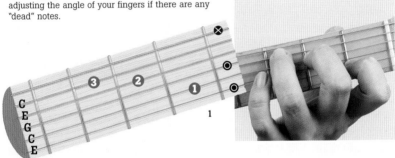

D

Check that the tip of your third finger is straight when you're fretting this chord. If it's leaning slightly, it could touch the top string and prevent it from ringing.

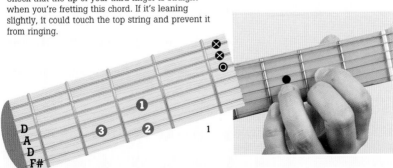

Lesson 7
Keeping the beat: clapping rhythms

Rhythm is king, period. Without rhythm there's no music; a strong beat without melody or harmony can still get people on the floor and dancing. So make sure you understand the rhythmic content of everything you play—if you can't clap it, you can't play it! You can use the accompanying CD to hear how a riff or melody should sound, but don't rely on it completely. If you get into the habit of clapping before you play, you can be certain that your playing will grow stronger and be more musical.

Rhythmic notation was discussed in Lesson 5 (see page 24), but it's worth glancing back to make sure you're clear about how to read the notes and rests before going any further. When you're clapping these exercises, aim to keep your foot tapping on the beat (this will require a bit of practice, so don't worry if you find it hard at first). The emphasis of weak beats (by the use of accents or rests) is called "syncopation" and is used in almost every style of music. The following exercises are designed to help you play notes "on" or "off" the beat so that you can syncopate with confidence. Start by practicing each bar separately and eventually you should be able to join both exercises together.

Example 1
Bar one uses rests to emphasize the strong beats one and three. In bar two, the rests are switched so that you clap on the weak beats two and four. This is called a "back beat" and it's the rhythmic foundation of popular music.

Example 2
The first bar is filled with eighth notes so you clap two notes on every beat. The second bar is harder because rests are added to create syncopation. Start slowly and don't forget to count the "+" after each beat—this is where the offbeat falls.

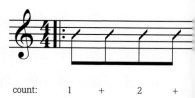

Repeat bars

A thick line followed by a thin line and two dots indicates a repeat. Always repeat whatever is between these two repeat markers (this can be several bars long).

Top tip

Practicing with a metronome (some electronic tuners have these already built in) will help you to develop a strong sense of rhythm and time more quickly.

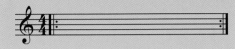

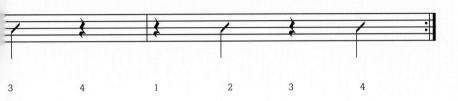

3   4   1   2   3   4

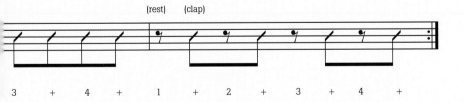

3   +   4   +   1   +   2   +   3   +   4   +

Lesson 8
Let's rock! Three easy riffs

What is a riff? In musical terms, it's an ostinato figure—a short, catchy, repeated phrase (typically no longer than two bars) that grabs the listener's attention and draws them into the song. Riffs are the building blocks of rock 'n' roll and no decent rock song is complete without one. For some examples of classic riff writing, listen to Deep Purple's *Smoke On The Water*, Green Day's *American Idiot*, Nirvana's *Smells Like Teen Spirit*, or The Rolling Stones's *Satisfaction* (the original rock riff—and one of the first to feature a fuzzbox).

The three riffs demonstrated below are all played on the sixth string. There are two reasons for this: first, low riffs are generally more effective than high ones; second, by playing all the notes on the sixth string, no tricky string jumps are involved, so you will be up and rocking in no time! Once you've mastered these riffs, you can play them to your friends—a good riff makes an ideal starting point for a jam session.

Easy riff: example 1
Keep your hand in third position throughout (i.e. with your first finger over the third fret); your third finger should then be hovering over the fifth fret.

Step 1

Before you start, make sure your hand is in third position (keep your first finger above the third fret). Although the first two notes are open strings, your fingers will be in position for the fretted notes.

Max up your practice

The best way to learn quickly is to start slowly and build up speed gradually. For the best results, use a metronome and start at a comfortable tempo—60 bpm is a good starting point.

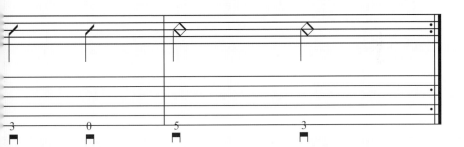

Step 2

Press down your first finger to play the sixth string note on the third fret. Try to keep your third finger hovering above the fifth fret ready for the next note.

Step 3

Play the fifth fret note by pressing onto the fretboard with your third finger. Ideally, only your fingers should move while your hand remains in third position.

Easy riff: example 2

*Watch out for the alternate picking
in this example. In the second bar,
because the first note is tied (it rings
from the previous bar and is therefore
not picked), the first "played" note
starts with an up-pick.*

Step 1

*This riff also starts with your hand
in third position ready to play the
fretted notes.*

Step 2

*Fret the third
fret on the sixth
string with your first
finger. The right hand should be
playing a down-pick.*

Lessons

Top tip

The rhythmic content of any riff is just as important as the notes. Make sure you can tap or clap the rhythm accurately before you play.

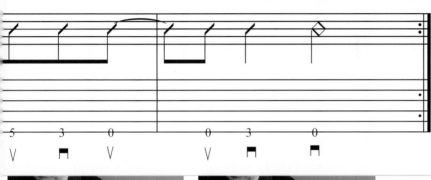

Step 3

Use your third finger to play the fifth fret on the sixth string. Your right hand should simultaneously be playing an up-pick.

Step 4

Keep your hand in third position as you return to the open string note. Your right hand should be playing an up-pick again.

Easy riff: example 3

This riff is also in third position, but you will need to move your third finger up to the eighth fret for the last pair of notes in the second bar.

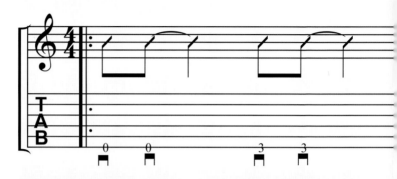

Step 1

As before, make sure your hand is in third position before you start the riff. All the notes in this riff are played with down-picks to create a driving rhythm.

Step 2

Simply press down your first finger to create the third fret note on the sixth string.

On the CD: tracks 2–4

All three of these riffs can be heard on the accompanying CD. Listen to them first while following the music through.

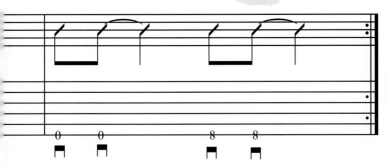

Step 3

While returning to the open string, move your hand up to sixth position (your first finger should hover above the sixth fret) so that you are ready for the following note.

Step 4

With your hand already in sixth position, all you have to do is press your third finger onto the fretboard to create the final pair of notes on the eighth fret. If you are repeating the riff, return your hand to third position while playing the first two open notes and repeat steps 2–3.

Lesson 9
Basic strumming patterns

By now you should have memorized the G, C, and D chords from Lesson 6—you're probably also getting a little bored with just changing between the three shapes. By strumming lightly across the strings with a pick, you can introduce some rhythm to those chord shapes and make them sound much more interesting. You've probably seen guitarists strumming before and thought that it looks very easy but, like most things that involve coordination, it can be tricky at first. The upside is that once you've mastered strumming, your playing will start to sound more professional and you'll be ready to impress your friends. Each example has been written with a G chord simply because this chord uses all six strings, so you can concentrate fully on the strum rhythm. Once you can play each exercise confidently, try playing a C or D chord instead of the G—just remember to avoid hitting any unwanted open strings with your pick (these have an "x" next to them on the chord box). As with all the exercises in this book, don't forget to clap through each example before you play it.

Example 1

This is a constant eighth-note strum using down and up strumming throughout. Notice that the down strums fall on the beat, while the up strums occur on the offbeats.

count: 1   +

On the CD: tracks 5–7

All three strumming rhythms are demonstrated with a G chord on the CD. Once you've played each exercise a few times, try playing along with the CD.

Strum direction

Alternate strumming shares the same symbols as alternate picking.

⊓ down strum

∨ up strum

Top tip

It's important to keep the wrist of your strumming arm relaxed—don't allow it to become tight. Each down and up movement should travel the same distance in order to maintain an even rhythm.

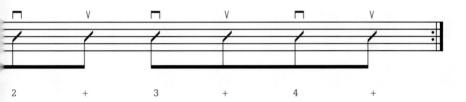

2   +   3   +   4   +

Step 1

This is how your pick should look at the start of the first up-strum. Keep the pick at 90 degrees to the strings and move it upward, gently brushing across all six strings.

Step 2

Immediately after each up-strum the pick returns to a down-strum. Don't make your strums too "wide"—it's easier to maintain a constant rhythm with small, precise strokes.

count: 1   +   2   +

Example 2

Keep your strumming hand constantly moving down and up in a pendulum-like motion. The up-pick does not make contact with the strings during beats one, two, and four—this is called "ghosted" strumming.

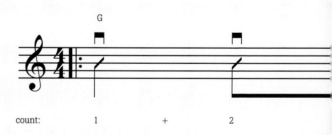

count: 1   +   2

Example 3

This example adds a ghosted down strum on beat three—these are much harder to play, so don't worry if you find this difficult. Start slowly and make sure you keep counting.

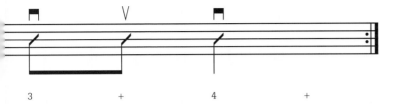

3   +   4   +

Step 1

Start the first down-strum with your pick at 90 degrees. Try to return to this exact spot at the end of the "ghosted" up-strum.

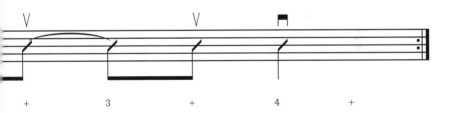

+   3   +   4   +

Step 2

This is where your pick should be at the start of the up-strum on beat two. Keep your hand moving in the same rhythm as before when you play the "ghosted" down-strum that follows.

Lesson 10
More chords

This lesson explains the two remaining open major chord shapes, plus two open minor chords. These chords are referred to as "open" because all the chords you have learned so far consist of fretted notes and open strings—the term "open" simply distinguishes these shapes from moveable chords that contain no open strings (more on these later).

Lesson 6 showed you the chords of G, C, and D. If you add to these the chords of E and A, you will have learned five very important chords—the five open shapes that all other guitar chords are derived from. And if that's not enough, you will also be adding to your rapidly expanding chord vocabulary the chords of E minor and A minor. As with major chords, the "minor" is abbreviated to simply an "m" placed after the chord, so that E minor is normally written as "Em" (or sometimes "Emin").

Top tip

Remember to keep your fingers as close to the frets as possible—if you don't place your fingers immediately behind the frets, the notes become harder to play and may also sound "buzzy."

E

You must ensure that you're not damping the important third string note by inadvertently touching it with your third finger. Keeping your fingertips angled at 90 degrees from the fingerboard is essential.

Lessons

A

This chord can be a little tricky with all three fingers squeezed into one fret—try juggling your fingers so that your third finger is closest to the fret, your second a fraction further back, and so on. The open sixth string should not be sounded.

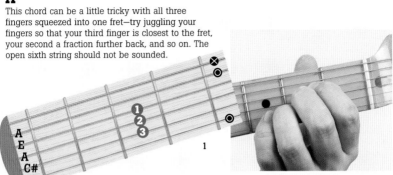

Em

This shape is the same as E major but minus the first finger. As with the E chord, ensure that the third string is ringing clearly (this note defines whether the chord is major or minor, so it's important that it's ringing).

Am

This shape is identical to E major except that it has been shifted over one set of strings so that each finger is placed a string higher. Notice that the open sixth string should not be sounded.

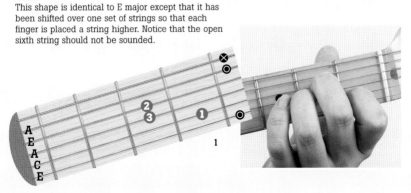

Lesson 11
Basic fingerpicking patterns

Using the thumb and fingers to pluck the strings is called "fingerpicking" and it's an exciting technique that opens up a whole new world of possibilities. It's not just popular with acoustic guitarists and singer/songwriters either; many electric players also eschew the pick in favor of fingerstyle technique and the softer tone and greater flexibility that it brings (Jeff Beck and Mark Knopfler are just two famous users of the technique). Some players grow their fingernails or use a combination of thumb and finger picks to achieve a bigger sound, but this is not really necessary for learning the basic techniques.

There are no hard-and-fast rules regarding the fingerpicking style, but generally you should use your thumb (p) to play the bass notes (the lowest three strings), and your index finger (i), middle (m), and ring (a) fingers for the melody notes. Whenever you're trying a fingerpicking pattern for the first time, play the parts separately—i.e. practice the bass line and then the melody, before you play both together. This is an efficient and more accurate way to learn.

Example 1
There are no fretted notes to worry about in this example. If you play the open strings as indicated, a simple E minor chord will result. Notice the pinch (bass and melody notes played together) on beats one and three.

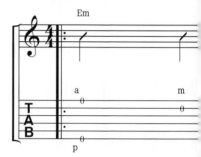

Step 1

The first pinch is played with your thumb (p) and your third finger (a). Notice the "claw shape" of the right hand—keep your fingers at 90 degrees from the strings.

Top tip

Keep your hand still so that all the movement occurs in your fingers. They should be bent at the first knuckle so you can pick away from the strings without your hand moving.

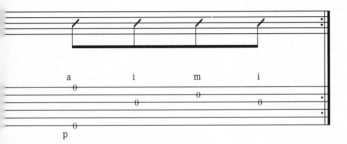

Step 2

The second note is picked with your second finger (m). Keep your thumb close to the sixth string without touching it.

Step 3

Use your first finger (i) to pick the third string. Keep your remaining fingers and thumb hovering above the strings without allowing them to make contact.

Example 2

*The right hand picks the same pattern
as in the second half of example 1,
this time over a full Em chord and
with additional bass notes. Notice
that the pinches fall on the beat and
are always followed by the open G
on the offbeats.*

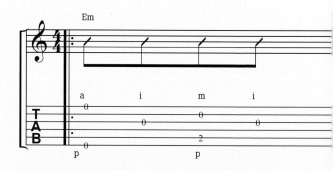

Step 1

*As in example 1, use your thumb (p)
and third finger to play the pinch on
beat one.*

Step 2

*Immediately following the pinch, use
your first finger (i) to pick the open
third string.*

The "pima" finger system

Traditional Spanish names are used to name the right-hand fingers—
using numbers would create confusion with the fretting hand.

p (pulgar) = thumb   m (medio) = middle
i (indice) = index   a (anular) = ring

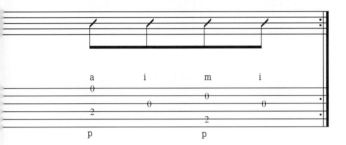

Step 3

For the second pinch, move your
thumb onto the fifth string,
simultaneously playing the higher
note with your second finger (m).

Step 4

When playing the third pinch on beat
three, move your thumb (p) onto the
fourth string and pinch the first string
with your third finger (a).

Example 3

Because the melody notes occur mainly on the offbeats in this pattern, it's harder to practice each part separately—try starting with the bass notes (played with the thumb) and gradually add the melody a note at a time.

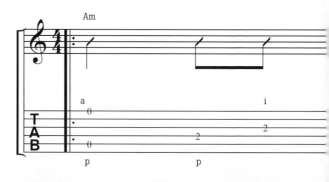

Step 1

Play the first pinch on beat one with your thumb (p) striking the fifth string while your third finger (a) picks the first string.

Step 2

Beat two starts with a single bass note on the fourth string. Play this note with your thumb (p).

On the CD: tracks 8–10

All three picking patterns are
demonstrated on the CD. Once you can
play each exercise confidently, try
playing along with them.

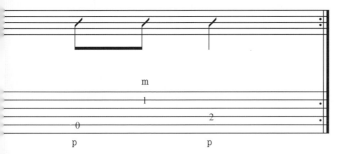

Step 3

Immediately after playing the fourth
string bass note, pick the third string
with your first finger (i).

Step 4

After playing the fifth string with your
thumb on beat three, use your second
finger (m) to pick the second string.

Lesson 12
Three chord progressions

There's little point in learning a group of chords if you're not going to play any songs with them, but it can be a daunting prospect trying to learn a whole song from one of those intimidating song books that often have multiple staves of music to navigate, with only a scattering of tiny chord boxes perched on top. The best way to memorize songs is in sections, starting with the verse, then the bridge, and finally the chorus. With that in mind, the following three examples are bite-sized, four-bar chunks of well-used chord sequences. These are ideal for practicing all the chords you've learned so far, and you can play them using your favorite strumming and fingerpicking patterns from Lessons 9 and 11. When you try these progressions for the first time, play each chord on the first beat only. You then have three beats before you hit the next chord in the following bar (it is best to practice with a metronome). Once you can do this, you can gradually introduce the strumming and picking patterns.

Example 1
This "three-chord trick" sequence uses the major chords learned in Lesson 6 (see page 26). When playing the progression strumming style, make sure you don't hit the unwanted open strings contained in the C and D chords.

Example 2
This sequence shifts between major and minor chords to create a darker, more "moody" accompaniment. Make sure you don't sound the sixth string when playing the C chord.

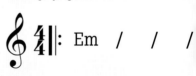

Example 3
The A minor and E chords use exactly the same fingering shape, so for a quick and easy change keep the shape intact when changing from E back to Am.

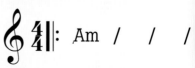

Top tip

The fingerpicking pattern in no. 3 is ideal for playing these progressions, provided you change two bass notes: for G and Em move the lowest bass note from the fifth to the sixth string. For the D chord, reverse the bass pattern so that you start on the fourth string. Listen to the CD if you're not sure.

On the CD: tracks 11–16

Each chord progression is demonstrated on the CD, first with strumming pattern no. 3 and then with fingerpicking pattern no. 3.

C / / / |G / / / |D / / / :‖

C / / / |Em / / / |G / / / :‖

C / / / |D / / / |E / / / :‖

Lesson 13
The minor pentatonic scale

The minor pentatonic scale is the most frequently used of all the scales. It occurs in blues, rock, country, and jazz, so it is only right that you should learn this scale first.

Penta is Greek for "five," and the term "pentatonic" is used to describe any five-note scale (there are many different types). However, it is the minor pentatonic that is vitally important to guitarists, since it is not only used to create riffs and chord progressions but, more importantly, solos; it is with this scale that most players take their first improvising steps. Scales are described in terms of intervals, which makes them easier to understand in musical terms.

The minor pentatonic is constructed as follows: 1 (root note); ♭3 (minor third); 4 (perfect fourth); 5 (perfect fifth); ♭7 (minor seventh). The table opposite explains how these intervals relate to frets on the guitar. All the exercises should be played in first position—i.e. play the second fret notes with your second finger and third fret notes with your third finger.

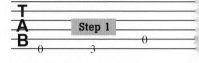

Example 1
A one-octave E minor pentatonic scale (octave = root note, eight notes higher—remember there is no F or C in this scale). The last note is the octave E, which is played once before immediately descending.

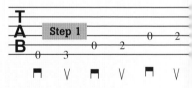

Example 2
A two-octave E minor shape one pentatonic (there are five basic shapes for each scale). Make sure you use the alternate picking as indicated (scales are the ideal vehicles for practicing your picking technique).

Max up your practice

Try singing each note before you play it— this will really help to internalize the sound of the scale and accelerate the development of your musical ear.

Lessons

Intervals

♭3	=	minor third (3 frets)
4	=	perfect fourth (5 frets)
5	=	perfect fifth (7 frets)
♭7	=	minor seventh (10 frets)

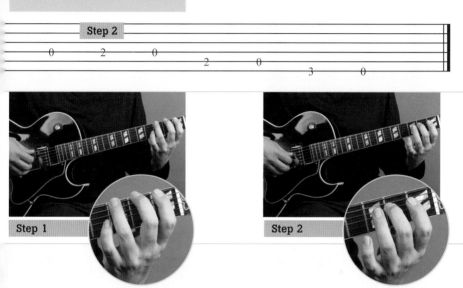

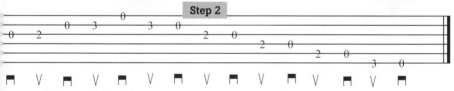

Lesson 14
Three pentatonic riffs

Now it's time to play some cool riffs based on the E minor pentatonic. Unlike the riffs in Lesson 8 that were all on one string, these riffs are played across several strings. The main advantage of this approach is that a wider choice of notes is available in a span of just a few frets. The following three riffs use syncopation, which makes the music interesting. (Since most riffs consist of only a few notes, syncopation is essential.) Make sure you can clap each riff before you try playing it (don't forget to count the beats). If you get stuck with the rhythm, listen to the CD, but remember that it's much better to understand the rhythm rather than just copying what you hear. As with the minor pentatonic scales, these riffs should be played in the first position. Once you've mastered these riffs, you could try writing some of your own.

Example 1
Don't forget that a tied note sounds for the sum of the two notes, so the fourth note in the first bar should start on the "+" of beat two and ring until the "+" of beat four, where the next note starts.

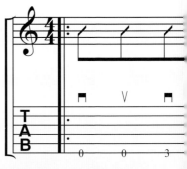

Step 1

The open sixth string is played twice on beat one— the second time with an up-pick.

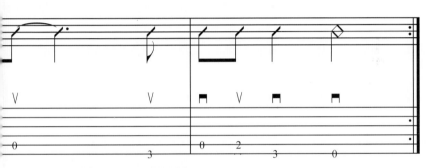

Step 2

*Bar two also
starts with
alternate picking—
use an up-pick for the second note.*

Example 2

String changes with alternate picking are tricky. Try to keep your pick between the two strings so that a down pick plays the higher string and an up pick plays the lower one.

Step 1

While picking the open second string on beat two, keep your second finger hovering above the fifth string ready for the next note.

Top tip

Practicing with a metronome is essential for developing a good sense of rhythm. Set your metronome at 60 bpm and gradually increase the speed (this may take several days) until you reach 100 bpm.

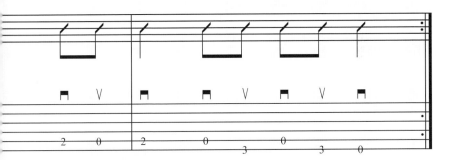

Step 2

This picture shows the open fifth string being played on beat two of the second bar. Keep your third finger hovering above the third fret ready for the next note.

Example 3

*This riff is heavily syncopated, so clap it
carefully before you try playing it. You
should clap on the "+" of each beat
from the second beat of bar one to the
second beat of bar two.*

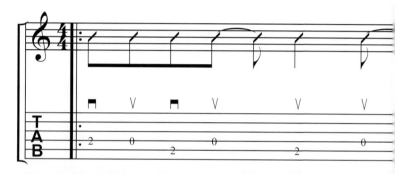

Step 1

*The second
note (open fourth
string) is played
with an up-pick. Make sure your
second finger is in position for the
fretted fifth string note that follows.*

Step 2

*Although the
fifth note in the
first bar is a quarter
note, it occurs on an off-beat ("3 +").
Make sure you use an up-pick
as illustrated.*

Lessons

On the CD: tracks 17–22

Each riff is demonstrated on the CD at two different tempos. The first is at 60 bpm, the second at 100 bpm—the tempo the riff should finally be played.

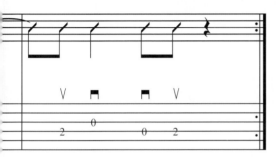

Step 3

The first note in the second bar falls on the "+" of beat one. Fret the note with your second finger and use an up-pick as illustrated.

Step 4

The last note of this riff is played with your second finger and picked with an up-pick.

Lesson 15
Climbing the neck: barre chords

Barre chords are different from the chords studied so far. They are moveable shapes, contain no open strings, and can be played anywhere on the instrument's neck. They are also more difficult to play since the first finger applies a constant pressure across five or all six strings. However, once you've mastered these shapes, you'll feel like a professional player—no longer will unusual chords such as B♭ or F# defeat you.

Since the lowest note denotes the chord's name, you will need to be familiar with the notes on the fifth and sixth strings, so now is a good time to check the fingerboard diagram on pages 10–11. Barre chords are generally easier to fret when moved up the neck, so practice them first wherever your fingers feel most comfortable (the fifth fret is a good place to start, giving you A major using example 1). Finally, don't be discouraged if these chords don't work straight away. Everyone finds these shapes tricky; it will be difficult to get all the strings to ring cleanly until you've built up the finger strength in your left hand.

Top tip

Practicing frequently in short bursts is the best way to build up your technique. So when you're watching TV, you could practice a few barre chords during the advertisements.

Barre type

A "type 1" barre chord is a six-string barre based on the open E chord shape. The "type 2" barre is a five-string barre chord based on the open A shape.

Lessons

Major—type 1

A full six-string major barre. Your first finger should be placed flat across the fretboard as close as possible to the fret. Once you've added the other fingers, check that all the notes are ringing by picking each string individually.

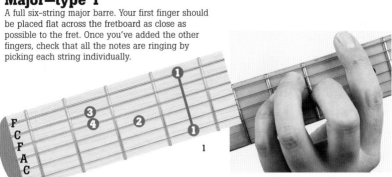

Minor—type 1

Omitting the second finger changes the chord from major to minor. It's important to check that the third string note rings clearly (adjust the position of your first finger if necessary).

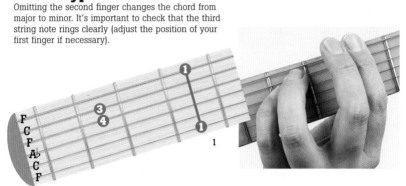

Major—type 2

This is a five-string chord, so the sixth string should not be sounded. A good way to prevent this string from ringing is to place the tip of your first finger just touching it, which will damp the string.

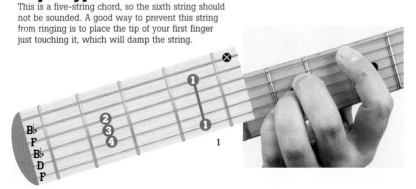

Lesson 16
All mixed up—barre chords and open chords

Sooner or later you'll come across a song containing an F chord. Even a three-chord trick in the key of C contains the chords C, F, and G, so it's likely you'll first start using a barre chord when an open chord is not available. Example 1 is typical of this situation. Once you're confident with the barre shapes, you'll probably find yourself substituting them for open chords because of the big, full sound they produce. The type 1, six-string barre is particularly suited to rhythm work. There are no open strings to worry about, so you can be as aggressive as you want with your strumming. Listen to legendary Stax house guitarist Steve Cropper's playing on the classic *Midnight Hour* or *Knock On Wood*. Both tunes were cowritten by Cropper and both open with descending type 1 barres that resolve to an open E chord. Example 2 mixes an open E chord with barre chords to create a classic chord sequence from this period. Sometimes a progression sounds better with barre chords. Example 3 uses five- and six-string barres instead of open chords. Take another look at the chord progressions in Lesson 12 and try playing them with barre chords.

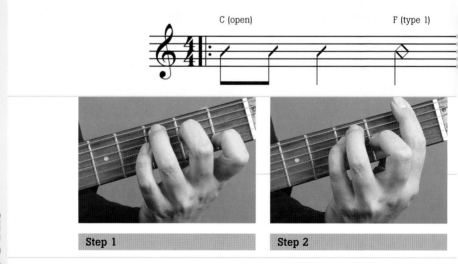

Step 1

Step 2

Top tip

When you're playing barre chords of the same type in succession (as in examples 2 and 3), simply release the pressure of your left hand and slide the shape along the neck to the desired fret (think of the strings as guide rails).

Example 1

Try to avoid moving your fingers further than necessary—i.e. when you're changing from C to F, your first finger is already on the first fret, so all you need to do is flatten it. Your second finger moves a string higher and the third stays put.

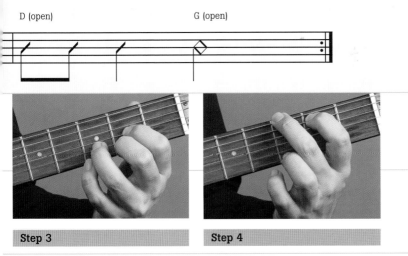

D (open)   G (open)

Step 3   **Step 4**

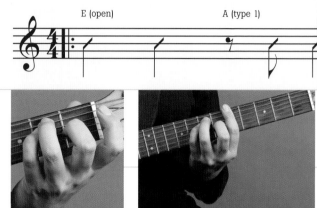

E (open)　　　　　　　　　　A (type 1)

Example 2

To change quickly from the E to a barre shape you need to change the fingering. By omitting your first finger and using your second, third, and fourth fingers, you can simply slide the shape up the neck and then add the barre with your first finger.

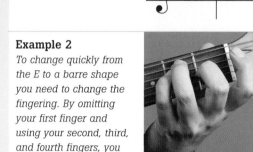

Step 1

Step 2

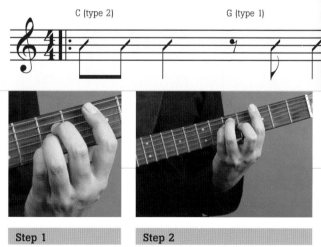

C (type 2)　　　　　　　　　　G (type 1)

Example 3

This progression starts with a five-string barre, so remember you will need to damp the sixth string by allowing your first finger to touch it (without actually fretting the note).

Step 1

Step 2

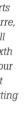

B (type 1)   A (type 1)

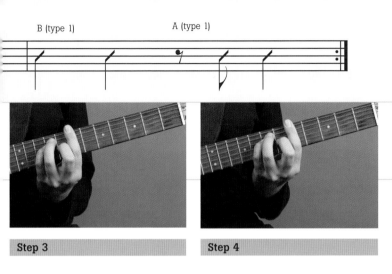

Step 3

Step 4

Am (type 1)   F (type 1)

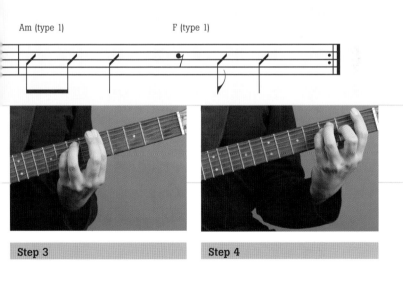

Step 3

Step 4

Lesson 17
Expressive techniques: bending and slurring

One of the big differences between a pianist and a guitarist is that a pianist is effectively playing notes by remote control; the guitarist, however, physically pushes down on the strings to create notes. This allows various expressive techniques to be used to alter the note's pitch or attack. These techniques are the tools that players use to stamp their personal signature on the music they play, and they can transform a string of mundane notes into an exciting piece of music.

String bending is a dramatic technique that enables the guitarist to emulate the most expressive instrument of all, the human voice. Bending a note changes its pitch by making the note sharper; releasing the bend allows it to return to its original pitch. The slur doesn't change the note's pitch as the bend does; instead, it changes its attack. Slurs come in three varieties: the hammer-on, the pull-off, and the slide. All of these achieve the same end result by changing the note's attack to produce a legato, liquid quality. These techniques, once mastered, will not only make your playing sound professional, but will help you to develop your own musical signature.

Example 1

As the note you start your bend on has no rhythmic value, you simply play the note and bend up to the bracketed pitch immediately. To bend down, don't repick the note but release it back to its original pitch. Use your first finger for the final slide (keep the fretting pressure constant as you slide).

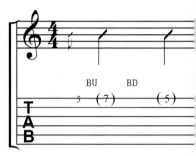

Step 1

Use three fingers for the two bends in this example. Your third finger actually frets the note (fifth fret)—the first and second fingers simply lend a hand!

Legend

5 (7) **Bend indication**: the first number is the fret you start the bend on; the number in brackets is the "virtual fret" you bend the note to.

Slur indication: when placed between two notes of different pitches, use a hammer-on to play a higher note or pull-off to play a lower. Only the first note is picked.

S **Slide indication**: slide up or down to the next note without repicking. As with hammers and pull-offs, only pick the first note.

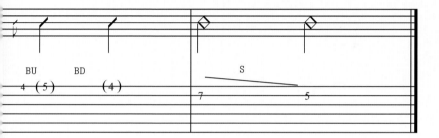

Step 2

To bend to the virtual pitch of the seventh fret you need to push the string upward as illustrated.

Step 3

Move your first finger up to the seventh fret (second string) in the last bar. After picking the note slide your finger back down the string to the fifth fret (don't lift your finger off the string).

Example 2

To play a pull-off to a lower note, flick your finger slightly sideways to sound the second note—it isn't picked. To hammer-on to a higher note, pick the first note only. The second note's sound is generated only by the impact of your finger hitting the fretboard—hence the technique's name.

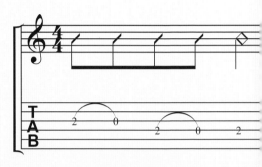

Step 1

Flick your finger sideways towards the fourth string to create the first pull-off.

Step 2

Fretting the third string in preparation for the pull-off to the open note.

Step 3

As you pick the first note in the second bar your second finger should be in position for the hammer-on.

Step 4

Fret the second string with your third finger, pick it and then slide up to the fifth (without releasing the pressure of your fretting hand).

Example 3

The arrow over the first note indicates a quarter-tone bend. This should be played with your first finger—you only need to bend the string very slightly. You can then play the fifth fret note with your third finger and the following slide with your second finger.

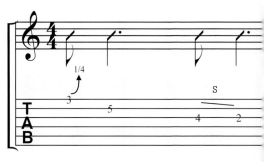

Step 1	Step 2
After picking the first note, push upward slightly toward the second string to create the quarter-tone bend.	*The slide in the first bar is played with your second finger—this keeps your third finger free for the next note.*

Top tip

Bends take a lot of finger strength, so use three fingers to execute the bend, with your third finger actually fretting the note. Always check the pitch you are aiming to bend to by playing it first—i.e. play the note in brackets before you bend to it.

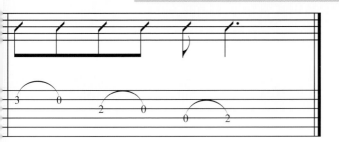

Step 3

The first pull-off is fretted with your third finger. Don't forget to flick your finger sideways as you lift it off the string.

Step 4

Make sure your second finger is in position for the hammer-on as you pick the final note.

Lesson 18
Three dominant seventh chords

It's now time to meet a very important member of the chord family—the dominant seventh. The seventh chord (as it's usually referred to) contains dissonance (this is the musical term for instability), which makes it a motion chord. It creates tension, which in turn creates harmonic movement. Traditionally, the dominant seventh was used as a V7 chord (refer to Lesson 6 where the I–IV–V chords in the three-chord trick were discussed) which resolved back to the I chord when a release from the harmonic tension was required. However, the widespread influence of blues and jazz, where entire chord sequences are frequently comprised of seventh chords, has meant that our ears now accept the seventh chord as a tonic (or I) chord. No self-respecting blues guitarist would use a straight major chord where a seventh would do. But even if the blues is not to your taste, the dominant seventh is a chord that occurs in every single style of contemporary music, so you will need to become fully acquainted with it.

Top tip

All these seventh chords contain one or more open strings that are important to the chords' quality, so make sure all the open notes are ringing clearly by picking each note individually.

E7

The basic version of this chord is just an E major
with the third finger omitted. However, most
guitarists add their fourth finger (in parentheses) as
this gives the chord a much stronger seventh flavor.

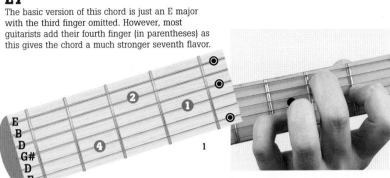

A7

Make sure you don't damp any open strings in this
shape—check the notes are ringing by picking each
string individually. Remember, your fingertips
should be 90 degrees from the fingerboard.

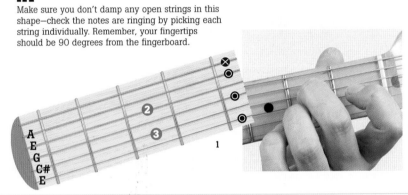

B7

Try not to include the sixth string in this chord—it's
a dissonant note and will not impress your friends.
Position your second finger so that it is closer to the
sixth string; it should then touch it slightly and
damp it.

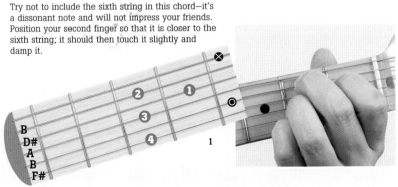

Lesson 19
It's time to rock 'n' roll!

When rock 'n' roll was born from the mixed parentage of blues, country, and jazz during the early 1950s, pioneering guitarists such as Bo Diddley and Chuck Berry often used simple riffs in place of the seventh chord. At the time this was probably seen as a "dumbing down" process, since the riffs used contained no third and so were neither major nor minor. However, the characteristic rock 'n' roll riff remains in use to this day ('70s rockers Status Quo built their entire career on it), and it was also the forefather of the power chord, which will be studied in Lesson 27. Although the riff is based on a quaver rhythm pattern, using down and up picking does not sound as effective as constant down picks, and these result in a much more driving, aggressive, and authentic sound. This is just one of the many stylistic techniques of '50s rock 'n' roll that live on in punk, rock, and heavy metal based styles to this day, confirming just how important this period was for the evolution of popular music, and the continued popularity and dominance of the electric guitar.

Example 1

Use your first finger for the note on the second fret. You should then be able to play the fourth fret note with your third finger. It's important that both strings are picked simultaneously.

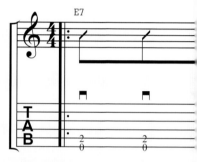

Step 1

While fretting the fifth string with your first finger, your third finger should be above the fourth fret ready for the next pair of notes. Use down-picks to play the chord.

Top tip

You can radically change the sound of this riff by palm muting with your right hand. Lightly rest the fleshy part of your palm on the bridge of the guitar where the bass strings join. By changing your hand position slightly, you can increase or decrease the effect.

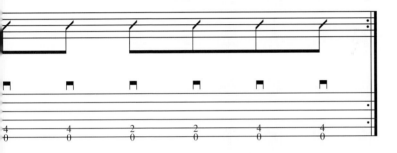

Step 2

As your third finger is fretting the fourth fret, aim to keep your first finger in position on the second fret. Down-picks should be used throughout.

Example 2

Use exactly the same fingering as in the previous example, but be careful not to play the unwanted open sixth string when you're picking.

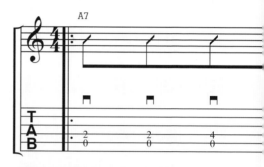

Step 1

The whole shape is shifted up a string for this riff. Fret the fourth string with your first finger while simultaneously picking the open fifth string.

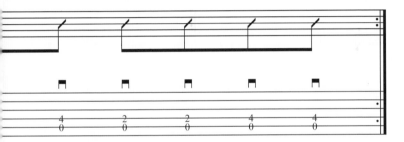

Step 2

As before, your third
finger frets the fourth fret
while your first finger remains in
position. To avoid hitting the open sixth
string, use short down-pick strokes.

Example 3

This is the moveable, fretted version of the previous two riffs and can be played anywhere on the fingerboard, just like the barre chords in Lesson 15. So if you find it a difficult stretch, try playing it higher up the neck.

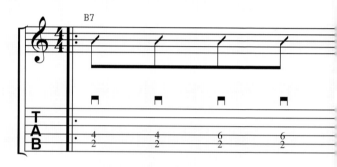

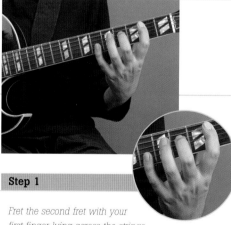

Step 1

Fret the second fret with your first finger lying across the strings. This will make it easier to fret the fourth fret with your second finger.

On the CD: tracks 23–28

All three riffs are demonstrated twice on the CD, the second time with a shuffle groove. Playing a shuffle groove is instinctive—it is not notated and basically involves swinging the quavers as a jazz musician would. Listen to the CD and see if you can play the riffs both ways.

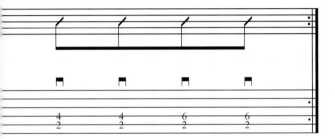

Step 2

With the first and second fingers remaining in position, fret the sixth fret with your fourth (pinkie) finger. Once again, use down-picks throughout.

Lesson 20
12-bar blues in E

The 12-bar blues is possibly the most ubiquitous chord progression in Western music. Although its roots are firmly embedded in the blues tradition, the chord sequence has been "lifted" and used in just about every other contemporary genre from jazz to the simplest pop music. For most guitarists, it's usually the first chord sequence they learn (some don't learn any other) and it's something that the professional musician will never escape; any self-respecting "function" band knows at least a dozen 12-bar rock 'n' roll tunes. Elvis Presley's early career was launched on the back of this harmonic vehicle. The Beatles used it, as did The Rolling Stones, Jimi Hendrix, and Led Zeppelin. It is seamlessly woven into the tapestry that is contemporary music. Example 1 demonstrates the basic chord progression (Roman numerals are given opposite to help you transpose this sequence to other keys later), while Example 2 is a full 12-bar melody. You can use the seventh chords shown in Lesson 18 (fingerstyle or strummed), or the rock 'n' roll riff from Lesson 19 for accompaniment.

Example 1
This is the traditional 12-bar blues sequence. Using Roman numerals as well as chord symbols makes it easy to transpose this sequence to other keys.

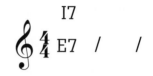

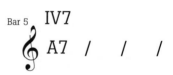

Roman numeral system

I7 = Dominant seventh on root

IV7 = Dominant seventh on fourth step
(count 5 frets up from your root note)

V7 = Dominant seventh on fifth step
(count 7 frets up from your root note)

/ | / / / / | / / / / | / / / / |

```
              I7
| / / / / | E7 / / / | / / / / |
```

```
IV7              I7                    V7
| A7 / / / | E7 / / / | / / B7 / ‖
```

Example 2
Bars 1–4

Your hand should be in the first position so that your third finger is fretting the first note (bend it slightly sharp). The slur sign means you pick the first note only and hammer-on to the next note if it's higher, or pull-off if the next note is lower.

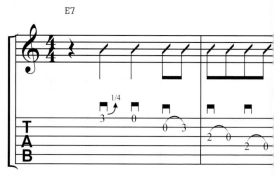

Step 1

Push the first string upward as you fret it with your third finger to create the quarter-tone bend.

Step 2

As you pick the second string on beat four, your third finger should be ready to hammer-on to the next note.

Top tip

All musicians use the Roman numeral system to describe chord sequences, which makes it easier to transpose progressions to other keys. This is usually done for the benefit of a singer or horns (saxophone or trumpet), or sometimes just because it sounds better in another key.

E7

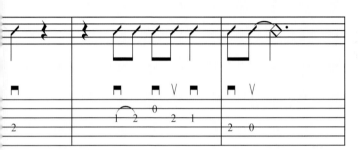

Step 3

Use your second finger for both pull-offs in the second bar.

Step 4

The hammer-on in the third bar starts on a fretted note. Make sure you keep your first finger in position as you hammer-on the second.

Bars 5–8

*At the end of bar seven, angle your
third finger slightly so that it just
touches the open E as you fret the
D on the string below (if both notes
ring together it can sound messy).*

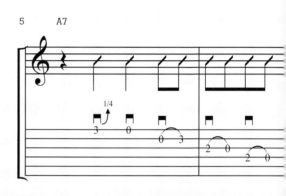

Step 5

*Use your third
finger for the
quarter-tone bend at the beginning of
the fifth bar.*

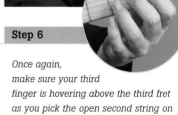

Step 6

*Once again,
make sure your third
finger is hovering above the third fret
as you pick the open second string on
beat four (bar five).*

Lessons

E7

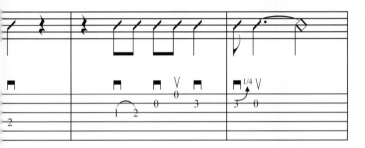

Step 7

Don't forget to
keep your first finger
in position as you play the hammer-
on in the seventh bar.

Step 8

Play the quarter-
tone bend at the
start of bar five by pushing your third
finger upward as you fret the note.

Bars 9–12

*The first note in bar nine should be
fretted with your second finger.
This will leave your third finger free
for the bend on the second string.
Don't forget that pull-offs sound
stronger when you flick your finger
sideways as you release the note.*

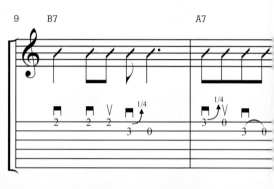

Step 9

Use your second
finger for the first
note in bar nine.

Step 10

The quarter-tone
bend in bar nine
should be played with your
third finger.

On the CD: track 29

Example 2 is demonstrated on the CD. The melody is panned left and the accompaniment is panned right. By adjusting your CD player's balance control, you can practice either part with the CD

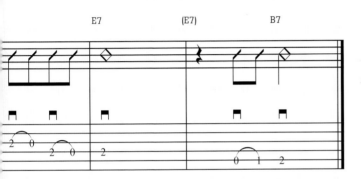

Step 11

Play the first pull-off in bar ten with your third finger. Don't forget that flicking the finger sideways creates a stronger pull-off.

Step 12

As you pick the open fifth string in the last bar, make sure your first and second fingers are in position for the last two notes.

Lesson 21
Just jamming: blues licks

The blues progression is great fun to solo over and a popular choice at jam sessions. However, improvising can be a daunting prospect if you've never done it before. What do you play? Where do the notes come from? The best way to start is by learning a few licks. Licks are part of the language of improvisation. When you talk, you use common phrases, popular expressions, and colloquialisms to get your point across. Licks function in much the same way; a skilled musician can mix them with scales, arpeggios, and spontaneous ideas to create an exciting solo. Most guitarists transcribe the licks of their favorite players; this is an important part of learning and helps to develop your "ear." Why not pause your CD player next time you're listening to your favorite guitarist soloing and have a go at copying a few notes?

Example 1

This Eric Clapton-style lick is based entirely on the Em pentatonic scale. The last note should be played staccato—cut the note short by lightly touching the third string with your first or second finger.

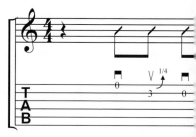

Step 1

Play the quarter-tone bend by pushing the string slightly upward with your third finger. Use an up-pick for this note as shown in the photo.

Staccato dot

A dot placed directly beneath or above a note indicates that it should by played short (staccato). You can stop an open string from ringing by damping it with your left hand, or keep a fretted note short by releasing the pressure of your finger.

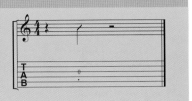

Step 2

Use your second finger to play the first note in bar two. Flicking the finger slightly sideways as you lift it off the string will create the open string note.

Example 2

*The late, great Stevie Ray Vaughan
was the inspiration for this lick, which
is based on the Em pentatonic scale.
The fourth note in the second bar is
borrowed from the blues scale (minor
pentatonic with added flattened fifth).*

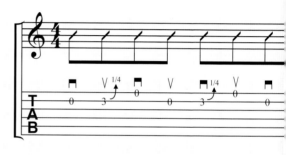

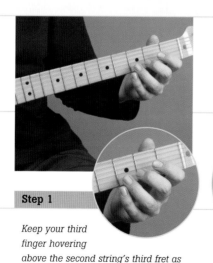

Step 1

*Keep your third
finger hovering
above the second string's third fret as
you play the first note—this will
enable you to move swiftly to the
following quarter-tone bend.*

Step 2

*Push the second
string upwards while
fretting with your third finger. Because
this bend falls on an off-beat it should
be played with an up-pick.*

Lessons

Top tip

These licks will work over any of the chords in an E blues progression (E7, A7, and B7). Once you've got them together, try playing along with the backing track from the previous chapter. You can add in your own ideas using the minor pentatonic scale from Lesson 13.

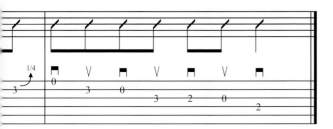

Step 3

Keep your third finger hovering above the second string as you play the open first string at the start of the second bar.

Step 4

As you play the third fret note on the third string, position your second finger on the second fret ready for the next note.

Example 3

Played higher up the neck in fifth position, this classic BB King-style lick mixes notes from the major scale with the minor pentatonic. Use three fingers for the bend in the second bar and cut the note short by releasing the pressure of your third finger.

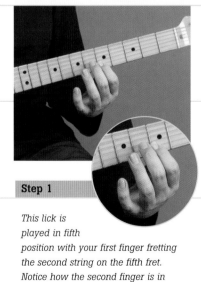

Step 1

This lick is played in fifth position with your first finger fretting the second string on the fifth fret. Notice how the second finger is in position for the next note.

Step 2

The third string is played at the sixth fret using your second finger— because it falls on an off-beat, use an up-pick.

On the CD: tracks 30–32

All three of these licks are demonstrated on the CD at 90 bpm. Try clapping along with the CD while reading the TAB before you try to play them.

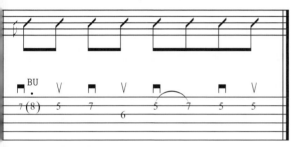

Step 3

Push the third string upwards with your third finger for the half-step bend at the start of the second bar.

Step 4

The hammer-on in the second bar is between two fretted notes. Before you pick the first note, make sure your third finger is hovering above the seventh fret.

Lesson 22
King of harmony: the major scale

The major scale is the foundation on which all harmony is built; it is the key to understanding how scales, chords, and arpeggios are constructed. The intervals that comprise this scale are all major or perfect, so when it is written in numeric terms (1−2−3−4−5−6−7−octave), there are no flats or sharps in front of the scale steps (e.g. like the ♭3 in the minor pentatonic scale). The pattern of whole steps (two frets) and half steps (one fret) remain constant whatever note you start the scale on, with the half steps always occurring between the third and fourth steps, and the seventh and octave. Both major and minor chords plus the all-important V–I perfect cadence are contained within this scale. In fact, the unique harmonic properties of this scale ensure its rightful place as the king of harmony.

Example 1

This one-octave scale is played in first position, so you start with your third finger and use your pinkie for the F# on the fourth string. You may find it awkward using your pinkie at first, but regular practice will soon make it seem easy.

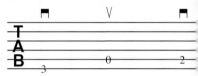

Step 1

Start the scale with your third finger on the lowest note. This should be played using a down-pick.

Top tip

The scales have been tabbed ascending only, but you should practice them ascending and descending without repeating the top note.

```
V           ■           V           ■           V
|-----------------------------------------------------------|
|-----------------------------------------------------------|
|-----------------------------------------------------------|
|-----------------0-----------------0-----------------------|
|-----------0-----------2-----------4-----------------------|
|-----3-----------------------------------------------------|
```

Step 2

The fourth note is also played with your third finger, this time on the fifth string. Notice how this note should be played with an up-pick.

Step 3

The penultimate note is played on the fourth fret of the fourth string. Use a down-pick while fretting the note with your fourth finger.

Example 2

The full two-octave major scale pattern adds the upper octave to the previous example. Once you can play it smoothly and without pauses, add the alternate picking as indicated.

```
       ⊓   V   ⊓   V   ⊓   V   ⊓   V   ⊓
   T ─────────────────────────────────────────
   A ─────────────────────────────0───2────
   B ──────0───2───3───0───2───4──────────
     3
```

Step 1

The two-octave major scale also starts with the third finger on the lowest note. Once again, use a down-pick.

Step 2

Use your third finger for the third fret note on the fifth string, playing the note with an up-pick.

Scale construction

W = whole step (2 frets or tone)

H = half step (1 fret or semitone)

1 – 2 – 3 – 4 – 5 – 6 – 7 – Oct
W   W   H   W   W   W   H

Interval checker

1 = root or tonic
2 = major second
3 = major third
4 = perfect fourth
5 = perfect fifth
6 = major sixth
7 = major seventh

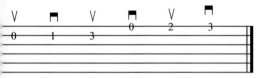

Step 3

Use an up-pick for the open second-string note. As you pick the note your first and third fingers should be hovering above their respective frets as shown.

Step 4

The highest note is played on the third fret of the first string using a down-pick.

Lesson 23
Short and sweet: major scale melodies

The major scale is the most melodic of all scales and provides the perfect note pool for creating tunes whatever the style of music, from simple folk songs to a full-blown symphony. During what many regard as the golden age of songwriting, the classic American songwriters (Cole Porter, Rodgers and Hart, Duke Ellington, and so on) of the 1930s and '40s often harmonized their major scale melodies with non-diatonic chords (these are chords that include notes not found in the scale). They realized that the major scale would create such a strong melody that it would easily withstand a bit of pushing and pulling harmonically. The following three melodies are all just four bars in length, but will hopefully illustrate what an effective melodic tool the major scale can be.

Example 1

Because this tune starts with a "pick-up" bar, the first note should be played with an up-pick. Notice that this pick-up phrase repeats at the end of the second bar.

Gone Fishing (Phil Capone)

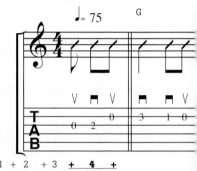

Step 1

The first note is shown correctly played with an up-pick and the second finger hovering above the second fret ready for the next note.

Pick-up bar

A pick-up bar is used when a melody starts before the first bar. The tune precedes the accompaniment by starting during the count in—in this case, on the "and" of beat three.

count: 1+2+3 **+ 4 +**

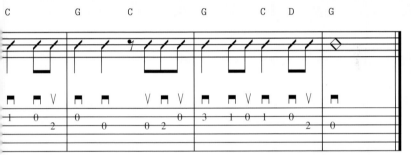

Step 2

The third note in bar one is the open second string, which should be played with an up-pick. Notice how the first finger remains just above the first fret ready for the next note.

Step 3

The second half of the tune (bar two, third note) starts with an up-picked open third string. The second finger is also above the second fret, ready for the next note.

Example 2

Your pinkie should fret the F# notes on the fourth string in the first and third bars. Aim to keep your fingers hovering as close as possible to the fingerboard and the notes they will be playing (this requires practice).

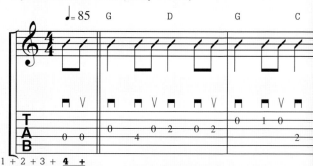

My Grandfather's Clock (Henry C Work)

Step 1

This shot shows the open third string being played with a down-pick, and the pinkie (fourth finger) in position above the fourth fret for the next note.

Step 2

Play the third note (open second string) in the second bar with an up-pick. Your second finger should also be above the third string ready for the next note.

Max up your practice

Don't forget that it's much harder to re-learn something once you've practiced it the wrong way, so take your time, start slowly, and clap along with the CD (while following the TAB) before you play.

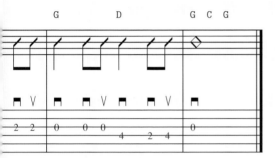

Step 3

In order to move smoothly between the second fret notes on the third and fourth strings, keep your finger flat and "roll" it across the strings to sound the notes separately.

Step 4

While playing the penultimate note in the third bar with your second finger, your pinkie (fourth finger) should remain hovering above the fourth fret.

Example 3

The pull-off in the pick-up bar will not work unless you fret both notes before you execute the pull-off. This will seem strange at first, but will become second nature with practice.

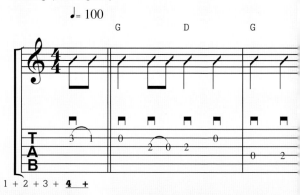

Sailing (Phil Capone)

♩ = 100

Step 1

In order to play the opening pull-off effectively you must fret both notes simultaneously, releasing your third finger by flicking it sideways.

Step 2

Keep your second finger hovering above the third string as you play the pull-off in the first bar—this will enable a quick return to the fretted note.

On the CD: tracks 33–35

Each tune is demonstrated on the CD with accompaniment.
As with the blues in Lesson 20, the rhythm guitar is panned
right and the melody panned left. By adjusting your CD
player's balance control, you will be able to play along with
the accompaniment only.

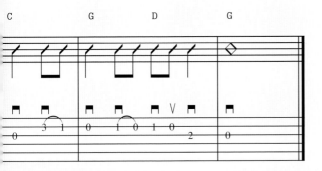

Step 3

*The third fret
pull-off is repeated
at the end of the second bar—make
sure both fingers are in position
before you pick the first note.*

Step 4

*Use an up-pick to
play the open
second string at the end of the third
bar; your finger should also be above
the second fret for the next note.*

Lesson 24
Relatively speaking: the natural minor scale

Minor tonality is more complex than major tonality because there isn't a "one size fits all" minor scale; there are, in fact, several different minor scales. Every major key shares its key signature with a minor key, called a relative minor. The natural minor scale (Aeolian mode) uses exactly the same notes as its relative major (other minor scales don't), so it makes sense to learn this scale first. To find the relative minor of any major key, all you have to do is count down a minor third (three frets) from your root note; the relative minor of G major is E minor. If we take the G major scale notes (G–A–B–C–D–E–F#) but start on the E, a very different interval formula emerges: 1–2–♭3–4–5–♭6–♭7–octave. Minor tonality is assured by the flattened third, while the flattened sixth and seventh heighten the dark, modal character of this scale.

Example 1

The one-octave natural minor uses the same three-note pattern on the sixth and fifth strings; use your second finger for the second fret notes and your third for the third fret notes.

Step 1

While playing the first note, move your second finger above the second fret for the next note.

Top tip

Don't forget to practice this scale ascending and descending (without repeating the highest note). Both scales should start and end on a down-pick if you use strict alternate picking throughout.

Step 2

The open fifth string should be played with an up-pick; notice that the fingers are also already in position for the next two notes.

Step 3

The last note is played with your second finger and an up-pick.

Example 2

The full two-octave scale incorporates the F# on the fourth string which should be played with your pinkie. Alternate picking should be added once you've mastered the correct fingering.

Step 1

Try starting the scale with your second and third fingers in position above their respective frets; this will enable you to achieve professional results quickly.

Step 2

As you play the second fret on the fourth string, try to keep your pinkie (fourth finger) as close to the fretboard as possible. This will speed up the note change and make the transition smoother.

Lessons

Scale construction

W = whole step (2 frets or tone)

H = half step (1 fret or semitone)

1 − 2 − ♭3 − 4 − 5 − ♭6 − ♭7 − Oct
W H   W   W H   W   W

Interval checker

1	=	root or tonic
2	=	major second
♭3	=	minor third
4	=	perfect fourth
5	=	perfect fifth
♭6	=	minor sixth
♭7	=	minor seventh

Step 3

It's difficult to get your pinkie to fret the string at a 90 degree angle, so don't worry too much if your finger appears "flatter" than the others, as in this picture.

Step 4

The open second string is played with an up-pick. The first and third fingers should also be in position above the string.

Lesson 25
Minor melody: *House of the Rising Sun*

Melodies written in a minor key are more melancholic and evocative than those written in a major key; if you play an open E chord and then hit an open E minor straight after it, you will hear how dark and sad the minor chord sounds when compared to its brighter, happier cousin. Remember that the natural minor scale also adds the minor sixth and seventh to create a dark, almost bleak landscape, creating the perfect atmosphere for the tune you're about to learn. *House of the Rising Sun* is a traditional folk ballad of unknown authorship and has been covered by many artists, most famously by The Animals in 1964. Both melody and accompaniment have been notated so you can learn both parts; the accompaniment can be played with a pick or fingerstyle—it's well worth practicing both techniques.

Example 1: melody
The following arrangement is a shortened version of the original folk classic. The Animals' famous recording of this tune was in A minor; this version has been transposed to E minor to make full use of the open strings and easy open chord shapes.

Step 1

Because it starts on an off-beat, the first note should be played with an up-pick.

Top tip

6/8 means there are six beats in every bar, but don't be scared—6/8 is a very natural rhythm. Once you've listened to the CD a couple of times, it will seem obvious. The important thing to remember is that an eighth note now equals one beat, so the pick-up note starts on beat six.

Step 2

Play the fourth string, fourth fret note at the end of the first bar with an up-pick—using your pinkie to fret the note.

Step 3

The open second string at the end of bar two is also played with an up-pick. Notice how the second finger is also hovering over the third string ready for the next note.

Top tip

If you're playing this with a pick, use the "three down" and "three up" sequence throughout; this will seem very natural once you get the hang of it. If you're playing fingerstyle, use the pima pattern indicated in the first bar throughout—simply move your thumb onto the fifth string for the five-string chords A, C, and B7.

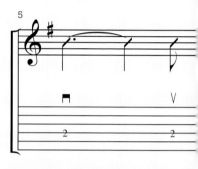

Step 4

Play the second fret note at the start of the fifth bar with your second finger, using a down-pick as illustrated.

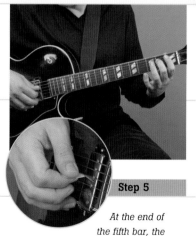

Step 5

At the end of the fifth bar, the second fret note is repeated—this time, played with an up-pick.

Lessons

Rogue note check

If you've spotted a rogue note in the tune, well done!
The first note in bar six (D#) is not from the E natural
minor scale. The seventh step of the minor scale is
frequently raised a half step to fit the dominant seventh
chord, which in this key is B7.

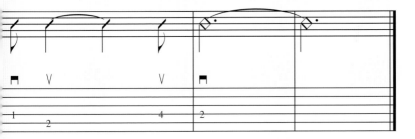

Step 6

The first note in
the sixth bar is
played with your first finger using a
down-pick. Notice how the second
finger is already over the fifth string
ready for the following note.

Step 7

The penultimate
note is on the fourth
fret of the fourth string, and played
with your pinkie using an up-pick. As
before, your second finger needs to be
in position for the final note.

Example 2: chords

1 *The unusual three-down, three-up picking pattern is used throughout the accompaniment. Avoid simply dragging your pick across the strings—remember, the picking pattern is also a rhythm.*

2 *An alternative fingering for the A chord uses a barre across the strings with the first finger. This allows quicker and easier chord changes.*

3 *When changing from Em to B7 (and vice versa), keep your second finger on the fifth string for a quicker change.*

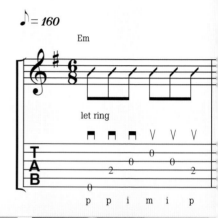

Step 1

Keep the Em shape fretted throughout the first bar, picking down on the sixth, fourth, and third strings.

Step 2

Jump to the second string and pick up the next three strings using up-picks. Keep the pick at 90 degrees to the strings as indicated.

Let it all ring out

"Let ring" is frequently written above the TAB when notes from a chord are picked in a particular rhythm, as in this example; simply hold the chord shape down and pick out the notes as indicated in the TAB.

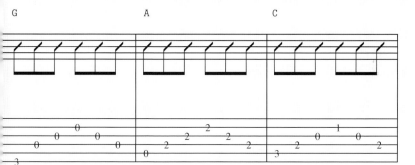

G   A   C

Step 3

Only the lowest two notes of the G chord are actually fretted. Using the same picking pattern, pick down across the lowest three strings starting on the sixth.

Step 4

The A chord when played with a first finger barre across the second fret. The picking pattern now starts on the fifth string with a down-pick.

Max up your practice

This accompaniment can be played with a pick or fingerstyle, so this is a great opportunity to practice both techniques with the CD.

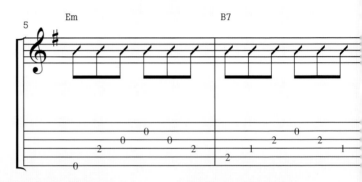

Step 5

Bar five is a repeat of the first bar with the picking pattern starting with a down-pick on the sixth string.

Step 6

Since the picking pattern does not extend to the first string, you can play a simplified B7 shape and omit the fourth finger. As with the A chord earlier, the picking pattern starts on the fifth string.

On the CD: track 36

The tune and accompaniment are demonstrated on the CD and, as with previous exercises, the tune is in the left channel with the accompaniment in the right. By adjusting your CD player's balance control, you will be able to duet with either part.

Em

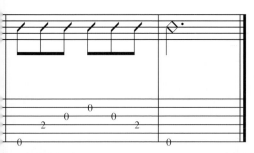

Step 7

The Em picking pattern used in this bar is the same as in bars one and five. Keep the chord fretted to allow the notes to ring clearly.

Step 8

With the Em chord intact and the notes still ringing from the previous bar, just pick the sixth string as the final note.

Lesson 26
Feeling the pinch: double stops

We first looked at double stops (pinches) in Lesson 11 as an introduction to fingerstyle technique. However, in this lesson we will look at how to play accompaniments based entirely on double stops, played either fingerstyle (as in Example 1) or with a combination of pick and fingers (as in Example 2), a technique known as "hybrid picking." Famous examples of tunes using a pinches accompaniment include The Beatles' *Blackbird* (played fingerstyle on acoustic by Paul McCartney), Mauro Giuliani's *Andante in C* (the theme tune to the Canadian kids' show Tales of the Riverbank), and The Red Hot Chilli Peppers' *Scar Tissue* (double stops are a trademark of Chilli's guitarist John Frusciante's technique). This invaluable accompaniment tool, as you will gather from the above examples, sounds great played on either acoustic or electric guitar.

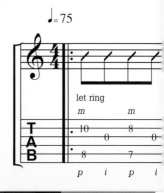

Step 1

Fret the first pinch using your first and fourth fingers. Your right hand "pinches" the notes using the thumb (p) and second finger (m).

Step 2

The second pinch is fretted with the first and third fingers. As before, use your thumb (p) and second finger (m) for the pinch.

Example 1

1 *The first double stop in this exercise is major; major pinches span three frets and should be played with your first finger on the fifth string and your pinkie on the second (use this fingering for all other major pinches).*

2 *The second double stop is a minor type; keep your first finger on the fifth string but change to your third finger for the higher note (use this fingering for all remaining minor pinches).*

Top tip

The picking pattern for Example 1 remains constant throughout: your thumb plays all the fifth string notes, your middle finger plays the second string notes, and your index finger picks the repeated open G. The p and arrow next to the final C chord indicates a sweep across the strings with your thumb.

Step 3

The open string pinch is played on the fifth string with your first finger fretting the higher note. Use your thumb (p) and second finger (m) for the pinch as before.

Step 4

It's quicker to climb the neck using your second and fourth fingers to fret this next pinch. Use the same fingers (p and m) for the pinch.

116

Slow down

The abbreviation rit. (short for the Italian term ritenuto) in the last bar of Example 1 indicates that the tempo should be decreased (2x means on the repeat only) as you approach the final C chord.

Example 2

1 Hold the pick as normal between your thumb and first finger but extend your middle finger (m) outward so that it can simultaneously pinch the second string as you pick the fifth.

2 Your first finger should be poised above the first fret on the second string as you pinch the two open strings on beat one of the second bar; this will enable you to execute a smooth hammer-on.

♩ = 80

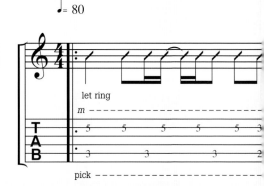

let ring
m - - - - - - - - - - - - - - - -
pick - - - - - - - - - - - - - - -

Step 1

The first pinch in this example is fretted with your first and fourth fingers. The pick strikes the fifth string while the second string is simultaneously plucked with the second finger (m) to create the pinch.

Step 2

As this double stop spans only two frets, use your first and third fingers to fret the notes. The pinch is played with the same combination of pick and second finger (m).

Lessons

Max up your practice

Although Example 1 is written for fingerstyle and Example 2 for pick and fingers, the techniques can be applied to either exercise, so don't be afraid to experiment.

On the CD: tracks 37–40

Both of these examples can be heard on the CD. Each example is played twice, first slowly and then up to the tempo indicated above the TAB.

Am

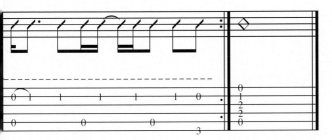

Step 3

Immediately after playing the open string pinch at the start of the second bar, hammer your first finger firmly onto the fretboard on the second string.

Step 4

This final pinch is a bass note on the sixth string (fretted with your third finger), and the open second string. Use your pick to strike the bass note while plucking the second string with your second finger (m).

Lesson 27
Metal mania: power chords

Power chords are definitely specific to guitar playing. If you ask any keyboard player to play you one, they will probably look at you blankly! The power chord evolved from the two-note rock 'n' roll riff explained in Lesson 19. Sometimes also played as a three-note chord, when notated its letter name is always followed by a "5." So a C power chord would be written as "C5." When guitarists started cranking up their valve amps in the 1960s, they noticed that certain chords sounded better with distortion than others. The presence of the third in "traditional" chords creates dissonance when played with distortion, while chords that omit the third create a wonderful, huge sound when played through a cranked up amp or effects pedal. The three most common types of power chord are moveable shapes with their root note on either the fourth, fifth, or sixth string, but there are also open versions—don't forget to check them out in the chord library at the end of the book. These chords are still widely used today and are essential for any self-respecting heavy rock, metal, grunge, or punk guitarist.

Top tip

The lowest note of each power chord is the chord's root note. So, as with the barre chords in Lesson 15, you will need to make sure you know your notes on not just the fifth and sixth strings but on the fourth string too. Don't forget the handy fretboard diagram at the beginning of the book (see page 10).

Max up your practice

Once you're confident with the shapes, practice changing between them. It's also a good idea to practice shifting the same shape up and down the neck—many riffs employ the chords in this way.

Lessons

Type 1: Root on sixth string

*Careful angling of the first finger will enable
you to damp the unwanted open strings by
gently resting your finger across them.*

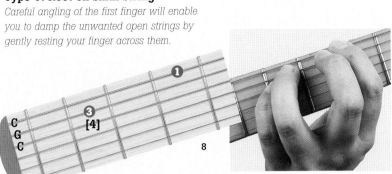

Type 2: Root on fifth string

*By damping the higher strings as in the
previous chord, you will also be able use the tip
of your first finger to damp the sixth string.*

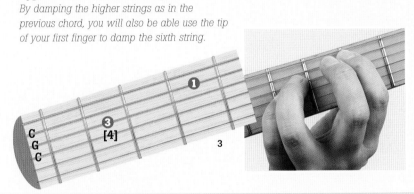

Type 3: Root on fourth string

*The three-note version of this chord spans four
frets; make sure your fingers are as close as
possible to the frets to avoid any muted strings
that don't ring clearly.*

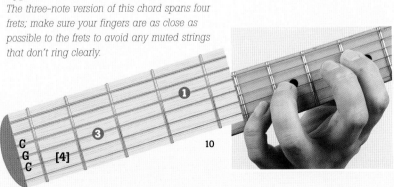

Lesson 28
Pentatonic chord progressions

During the 1960s, harmonic barriers (and many others) were challenged and popular music broke away from the restraining tonality of conventional major and minor harmony. It wasn't just musicians who were experimenting; mainstream songwriters such as Burt Bacharach and the Brazilian composer Antonio Carlos Jobim were also pivotal in stretching the boundaries of popular harmony. Chord sequences that are acceptable to our ears today would have sounded quite radical in the sixties. One way to create unusual chord progressions is to use the pentatonic scale to create a root movement. You can then use any chord type to harmonize the sequence, but major chords (or power chords) generally work best; there's something about major chords moving against a minor scale root pattern that sounds right in a wrong sort of way.

Example 1
Open major chords are used to harmonize a simple E minor pentatonic root movement.

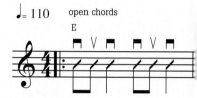

Example 2
Major barre chords (type 1 and 2) are used to harmonize another E minor pentatonic sequence that descends an octave from the E barre chord to an open E chord.

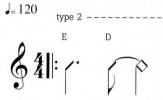

Example 3
This sequence starts on the ♭3 of the E minor pentatonic, alternating between six-string root barres (type 1) and five-string root barres (type 2).

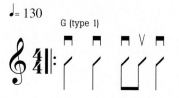

Max up your practice

Once you can play these sequences confidently, you could try them with the power chord shapes you learned in Lesson 27.

On the CD: tracks 41–43

All three progressions are on the CD. It's well worth clapping along with the recorded versions before you try them, as it will enable you to learn the sequences more quickly and accurately.

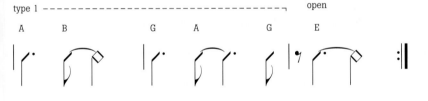

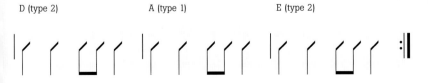

Lesson 29
Slave to the rhythm: damping

Damping or choking the strings to prevent them from ringing can be achieved with the right or left hand, and it's an invaluable technique for creating syncopated rhythms and spicing up your rhythm playing. Right-hand damping involves simply touching the strings with the side of your hand; by bringing your hand into contact with the strings more forcefully, you can also add percussive sounds to your accompaniments. Elements of left-hand damping were learned in Lesson 4 by muting unwanted open strings, but the technique can also be used to mute all six strings when you're playing barre chords. By releasing the pressure of the fretting hand the chord will be muted; strumming the damped strings will then create percussive rhythms. Bo Diddley was one of the pioneers of this technique in the fifties and it's widely used in many different styles, including funk, reggae, and rock to this day.

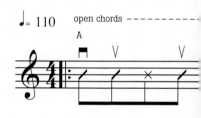

Example 1

Bring the side of your right hand forcefully in contact with the strings to create a drumming effect; this takes the place of a downpicked strum.

Percussive notes

Percussive notes simply have an "x" instead of a slash or notehead. In Example 1 this indicates where you hit the strings. In Examples 2 and 3, this is where you release the pressure of your fretting hand but keep strumming the strings.

On the CD: tracks 44–46

All three examples are on the CD. Listen to them carefully to make sure you know how the percussive notes should sound.

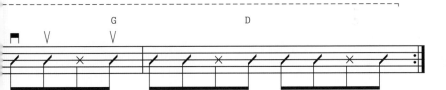

Step 1

This photograph shows the how to use the side of your right hand to hit the strings on beats two and four.

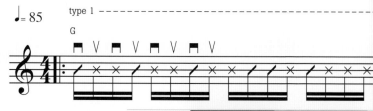

Example 2

Release the pressure of your fretting hand, but make sure you don't remove any fingers from the strings. The 16th note strumming pattern continues but is not heavily accented.

Step 1

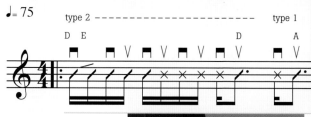

Example 3

This sequence starts with a D barre chord sliding up to E. The muted notes should be heavily accented. Notice that the single down and up strokes on beats three and four allow the chords to ring for the remainder of each beat.

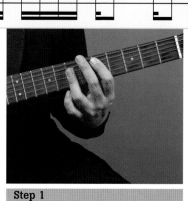

Step 1

Lessons

B♭   C

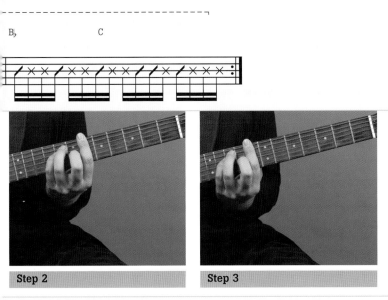

Step 2   **Step 3**

type 2 — — — — — — — — — — — — — — — — — type 1   type 2

D E   A   D

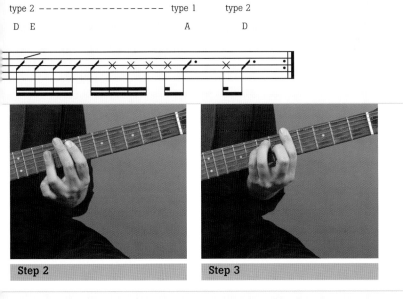

Step 2   **Step 3**

Lesson 30
Rock techniques: palm muting

Palm muting is most frequently used in rock styles and involves damping the strings with the heel of the palm placed on the strings near to the bridge. By touching the strings very lightly while simultaneously picking, a chunky, driving sound is achieved—perfect for power chords and low note riffs played with distortion. However, precisely where your hand is placed and how much of it touches the strings is crucial. If you apply too much pressure too far from the bridge, you'll just get a dull percussive noise; it's important not to stop the strings ringing completely. If you want to play rock, palm muting is invaluable; even if you don't, it occurs in many other styles too, so it's well worth getting together. Once you've found the "sweet spot" for positioning your right hand, you'll find this simple yet highly effective technique useful in many different musical situations.

Example 1
1 *Place the heel of your palm close to the bridge, allowing it to gently rest on the strings.*
2 *Your third finger should hover over the fifth fret while playing the first bar, which ensures a smooth, quick change to the fretted note.*

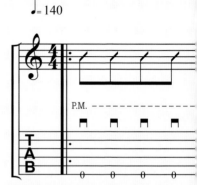

Step 1

Although this riff starts with the open sixth string, keep your hand in third position ready for the fretted notes in the second bar. Place the heel of your right hand palm close to the bridge, allowing it to gently touch the strings.

Palm muting

The letters "P.M." and a dashed line indicate that all notes or chords within this section should be palm muted.

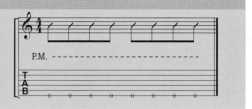

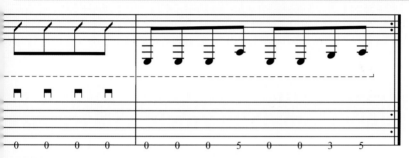

Step 2

With your left hand already in position, simply depress your third finger to create the fifth fret note in the second bar. Notice how the picking hand position remains constant with down-picks used throughout.

Step 3

To play the penultimate note, simply depress your first finger. Maintain the right-hand position and play the note using a down-pick.

Top tip

Remember that you should only be applying a very light damping pressure—the pitch of each string still needs to be heard. Practice the technique by starting with a slow down-pick and experiment with varying amounts of right-hand pressure and the distance of your palm from the bridge.

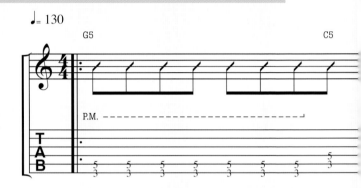

Example 2

1 *When playing power chords, make sure the heel of your palm is touching the lower strings (this is particularly important for the D5).*
2 *Lift your palm just off the strings to allow the C5 and D5 to ring, but keep your hand in position ready for the quick return to muting.*

Step 1

Palm muting a power chord is a little more tricky—apply even (gentle) pressure to both strings with the heel of your right hand, close to the bridge.

Lessons

Max up your practice

Using alternate picking while palm muting several strings is tricky. Start this example slowly at around 80 bpm, gradually notching your metronome up to the target speed of 130 bpm.

Top tip

To achieve a deeper sound and even attack, constant down-picks are used when playing heavy riffs and power chords.

D5

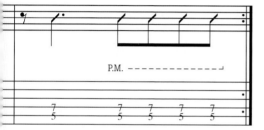

Step 2

The power chord moves onto the fifth and fourth strings at the end of the bar. Avoid picking the sixth string by starting the down-pick on the fifth string as illustrated.

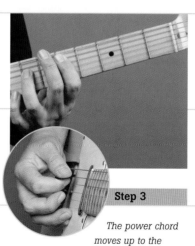

Step 3

The power chord moves up to the seventh fret in the second bar—maintain the right-hand palm muting pressure by keeping your picking hand still.

Example 3

1 *Palm damping chords with alternate picking is much trickier. Your palm needs to rest gently across the lower four strings with even pressure on each.*

2 *Don't bother playing a full Em chord. Simply fret the fourth string with your second finger, keeping your third ready for the added A note.*

One bar repeat

A dash flanked by two dots indicates a one-bar repeat. Simply repeat whatever was played in the previous bar.

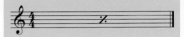

♩= 120

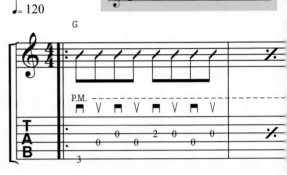

Step 1

The G chord in this example initially uses only the fretted third note with added open strings. Lay the side of your palm right across the bottom four strings close to the bridge.

Step 2

The second finger is added on the third string halfway through the bar. The alternate picking pattern now starts on the third string with a down-pick.

Lessons

On the CD: tracks 47–49

Listening to the CD will clarify how these pieces should sound when correctly palm muted. Example 1 is typical heavy rock palm muting. Example 2 is slightly more punky, while Example 3 is a pop riff played with a clean, chorused tone.

Em

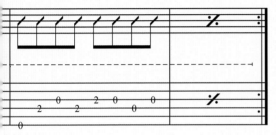

Step 3

Fret the Em chord with only the second finger on the fourth string. Start the picking pattern on the sixth string with a down-pick.

Step 4

The third finger is added to the chord on the third string. Once again the alternate picking pattern now starts on the third string with a down-pick.

Lesson 31
Changing keys: using a capo

A capo is a device for changing keys that you clamp onto your guitar neck and is fitted close behind the fret in the same way that you would fret a note. It has the effect of shifting the nut (or "zero fret") higher up the neck. Some players think using a capo is "cheating," but too much good music has been recorded with this great little tool to ignore it. Capos are most frequently used by fingerstyle guitarists to shift open chord sequences into a higher key, either for the benefit of a vocalist, or simply to make the guitar sound brighter and less bass heavy when playing alternating bass accompaniments. Many bluegrass, country, and folk musicians permanently play with a capo; singer-songwriters like Bob Dylan and James Taylor have also used them on many famous songs. Capos are available for acoustic and electric guitars, so it's well worth asking the advice of your local music store to make sure you get the right type for your guitar before you buy (see Buyer's Guide, pages 226-249).

Example 1: Capo 2nd fret
1 When attaching the capo, make sure it's snugly clamped behind the desired fret.
2 The G chord in the first bar has no root note or top note, so you only need to fret the fifth string with your second finger.

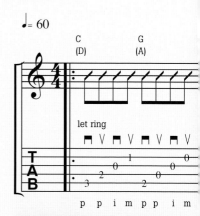

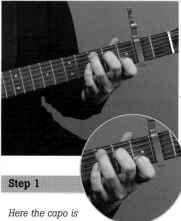

Step 1

Here the capo is placed on the second fret. Playing a normal C shape with the capo in this position means you are actually playing a D.

Lessons

Max up your practice

Example 1 can be played fingerstyle or with a pick. Example 2 is a strummed chord progression and Example 3 is a fingerstyle example. Try playing these examples with and without the capo so that you can hear the difference the capo makes.

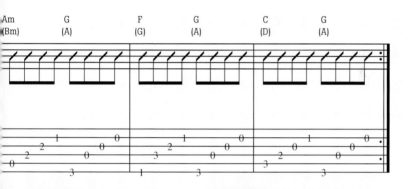

Step 2

Since the G chord only uses four strings, there's no need to fret all the notes. Just use your second finger for the second fret on the fifth string.

Step 3

The G chord used in the remaining bars only needs to be fretted on the sixth string with your third finger.

Example 2: Capo 7th fret

1 *Simply lift your pick away from the strings to play the ghosted picking.*
2 *The A chord in the final bar is played by barring across the second fret with your first finger. By angling your finger slightly you should be able to avoid fretting the first string.*

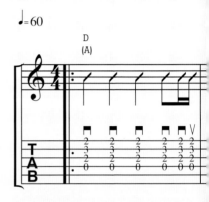

Step 1

With the capo at the seventh fret, a simple D shape creates a high A chord.

Step 2

Playing the C shape with the seventh fret capo creates a high G chord.

Lessons

Top tip

When songs are strummed at slower tempos as in Example 2, it's easier to keep time more accurately if you strum 8th or 16th notes with ghosted strumming. In this example, a 16th note ghosted strum pattern is played constantly, but the extra pick strokes only make contact with the strings at the end of each bar.

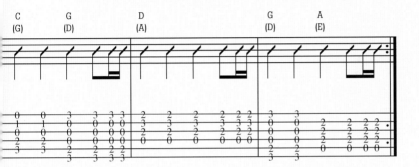

Step 3

Here the G chord shape is played with the second, third, and fourth fingers for a quick change from the C shape. The resulting chord is actually D.

Step 4

The A shape chord (actually a high E chord) is played by barring with the first finger only—it would be awkward using individual fingers this high up the neck.

Example 3: Capo 3rd fret

1 *As in Example 2, the A chord in this sequence is played with a first finger barre. However, there is no need to worry about damping the first string when playing fingerstyle.*

2 *When changing to the final E chord, don't wait until the chord is in place before you play the first pinch. These are open strings anyway, so the pinch and chord change can occur simultaneously.*

Top tip

When playing more complex picking patterns as in Example 3, try practicing the bass part on its own first and gradually adding the melody notes. The bass notes are the notes played with your thumb (p).

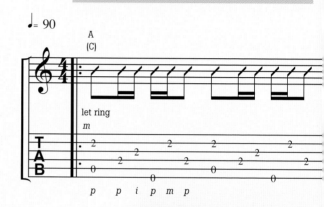

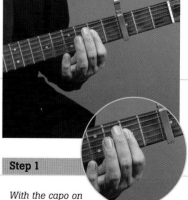

Step 1

With the capo on the third fret, playing an A shape (by barring with the first finger) creates a C chord.

On the CD: tracks 50–53

Don't forget to check out the examples
on the accompanying CD. Examples 1
and 2 are played at full tempo. Example
3 is played at two tempos—slow and
then full.

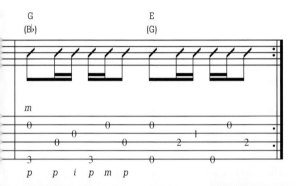

Step 2

Since the chord
is fingerpicked, you
only need to fret the G shape with
your third finger. The actual chord
created is B♭.

Step 3

A regular E shape
with the capo on
the third fret produces a G chord.

Lesson 32
Snakes and ladders: scale practice patterns

Practicing scales ascending and descending from a low root note is very useful for learning the scale itself, but it has little to do with playing melodies. It's not that scales are unimportant—they're an integral part of music making. However, in performance situations scales are rarely played in this way; phrases can start on any note and may involve interval jumps, string skipping, arpeggios—the possibilities are endless. So, to prepare for these demanding musical situations, musicians practice arpeggios and note sequences starting on each scale step. Practicing scales using this approach is also a good way to build up licks and soloing ideas; a simple note sequence can trigger an idea that becomes an interesting melody or phrase if your creative juices are flowing.

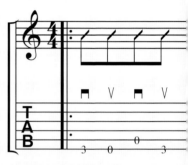

Example 1: E minor pentatonic
1 *By positioning your pick in the middle of the strings you will find the string jumps (e.g. between notes two and three in the first bar) much easier to execute.*
2 *While playing an open string, position your finger ready for the next note, as in the first two notes of the second bar.*

Step 1

Keep your third finger hovering above the fret when you lift it off to play the open string on beat one. This should also be played with an up-pick as indicated.

Max up your practice

No tempo indications are given for these exercises since they should only be played at a tempo that is comfortable for you. Always start slowly and try gradually increasing the tempo each time you practice, but don't play faster than you can play cleanly and accurately.

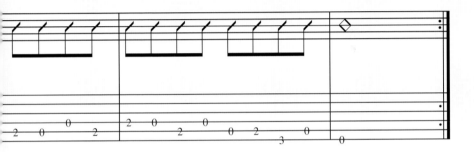

Step 2

The second time you play the sixth string on the third fret you should be using an up-pick.

Step 3

The highest note is played with the second finger on the fourth string before the pattern reverses and descends.

Example 2: E minor pentatonic

1 *To achieve an even and smooth delivery, keep your fretting fingers close to the fingerboard, even when playing open strings.*

2 *By lightly touching the open E string (second bar) after playing it, you can prevent it from ringing simultaneously with the following A (open fifth string).*

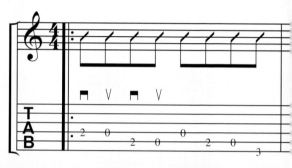

Step 1

Using strict alternate picking throughout, start with your second finger on the fourth string using a down-pick.

Step 2

The open fourth string is played with a down-pick on the third beat. Notice how the second finger has moved across to the fifth string ready for the next note.

Top tip

There are limitless combinations of notes that you can use to practice scales—these are just a few ideas to get you started. There are many excellent books devoted solely to scale practice if you are keen to explore the subject in depth.

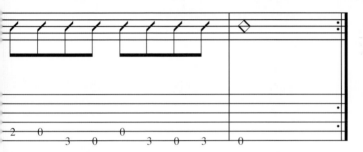

Step 3

The last note in the first bar is fretted with your third finger and played with an up-pick.

Step 4

The open fifth string on beat three of the second bar is played with a down-pick, while you simultaneously prepare your third finger for the next note.

Example 3: G major scale

1 *Position your fourth finger just above the fourth fret while you play the open fourth string (second bar).*

2 *Changing from your second to your fourth finger is always tricky. Try to stretch out your pinkie as much as you can while playing the last note of the second bar.*

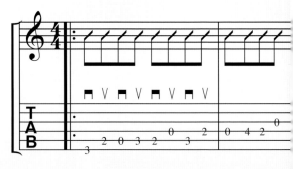

Step 1

This pattern starts on the sixth string with your third finger fretting the third fret.

Step 2

Pick the open fourth string in the first bar with an up-pick while you position your third finger over the fifth string for the following note.

Top tip

Playing a few simple exercises is the best way to warm up your fingers and improve your right- and left-hand coordination.

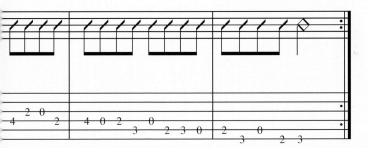

Step 3

Play the fourth fret, fourth string with your pinkie. The second finger should remain over the second fret for a quick change to the following note.

Step 4

The following fourth fret note moves straight to the third string, second fret. This tricky move involves good independence between the fingers and may take a little practice.

Lesson 33
Songwriting workshop: common chord progressions

Although each new musical movement claims that their music is new and totally original, only a few exceptional examples really are, and even those will be fully aware of music's vast history and heritage. Jazz genius Charlie Parker based many of his famous bebop tunes on the chord progressions of earlier standards; Led Zeppelin's pioneering heavy metal sound owed much to the riffs and chord sequences of early black blues musicians such as Blind Willie Johnson and Sonny Boy Williamson; Kurt Cobain admitted that the dark sound of seventies heavy metal band Black Sabbath was a big influence on Nirvana's grunge style. So it goes without saying that you can learn an awful lot about music by studying what works. The following chord sequences are not clichés to be avoided, but are intended to inspire both the budding songwriter and aspiring improviser. Like everything else in this book, you will gain maximum benefit by playing the exercises in different styles and tempos. Enjoy!

Example 1: E minor

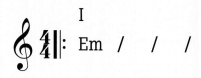

Example 2: E minor

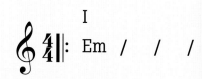

Example 3: E minor

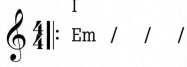

Top tip

Roman numerals are also provided to indicate which note of the parent scale the chord is based on. This system was described in Lesson 20 to explain the 12-bar blues, a system used by musicians to make transposing to other keys easier.

Max up your practice

You can also use these progressions to practice the chord shapes you have learned in this book, or try out new ones by referring to the chord library at the back of the book.

IV	I	V
|Am / / /	|Em / / /	|B7 / / / :||

♭VII	♭VI	♭VII
|D / / /	|C / / /	|D / / / :||

♭III	IV	IVm
|G / / /	|A / / /	|Am / / / :||

Top tip

Although these examples have been written with conventional major and minor chord symbols, they will also sound cool with power chords.

Example 4: G major

$$\text{I}$$
$$\&\, \mathbf{\frac{4}{4}} \|\!: \text{G} \quad / \quad / \quad /$$

Example 5: G major

$$\text{I}$$
$$\&\, \mathbf{\frac{4}{4}} \|\!: \text{G} \quad / \quad / \quad /$$

Example 6: G major

$$\text{IV} \qquad \text{V}$$
$$\&\, \mathbf{\frac{4}{4}} \|\!: \text{C} \quad / \quad \text{D} \quad /$$

Example 7: C major

$$\text{I}$$
$$\&\, \mathbf{\frac{4}{4}} \|\!: \text{C} \quad / \quad / \quad /$$

Example 8: C major

$$\text{I}$$
$$\&\, \mathbf{\frac{4}{4}} \|\!: \text{C} \quad / \quad / \quad /$$

Example 9: F major

$$\text{I}$$
$$\&\, \mathbf{\frac{4}{4}} \|\!: \text{F} \quad / \quad / \quad /$$

Max up your practice

Try changing the amount of time alloted to each chord. For instance, Example 1 could be a two-bar progression with two beats on each chord; or two bars of Em, one bar of Am, and two beats each on Em and B7. Nothing is set in stone, so don't be afraid to experiment.

V		II	
D / / /		Am / / /	Am / / / :‖

VI		IV		V	
Em / / /		C / / /		D / / / :‖

I	III7	IV	V	I	
G / B7 /		C / D /		G / / / :‖

♭VII		IV		I	
B♭ / / /		F / / /	C / / / :‖

V		VI		IV	
G / / /		Am / / /	F / / / :‖

IV		♭III		♭VI	
B♭ / / /		A♭ / / /	D♭ / / / :‖

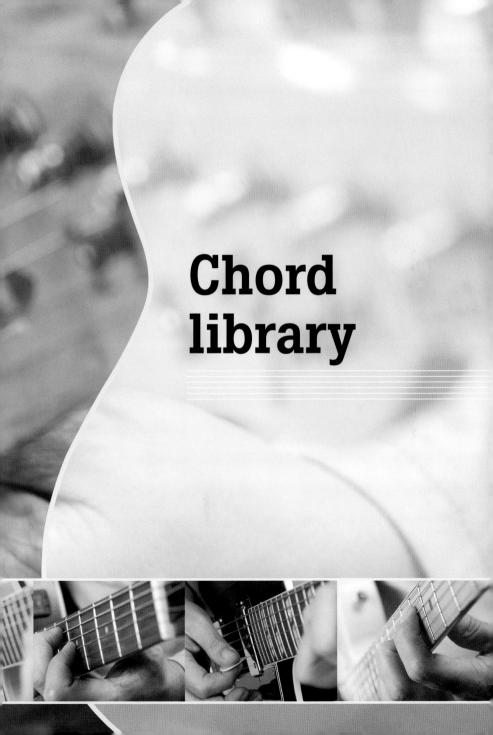

Chord
library

C

1 C major

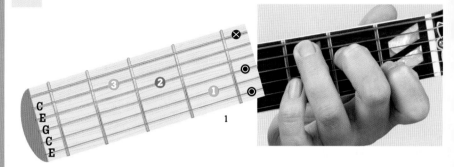

1 C minor

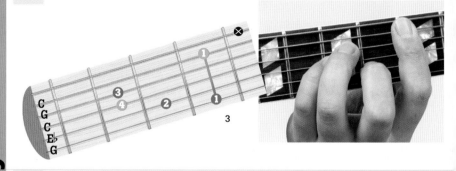

1 C7

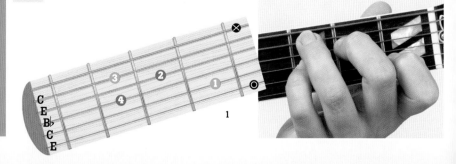

2 C major

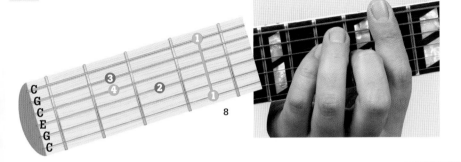

2 C minor

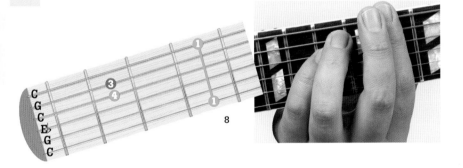

2 C7

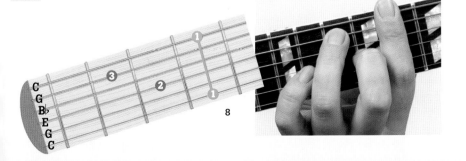

C♯/D♭

1 C♯/D♭ major

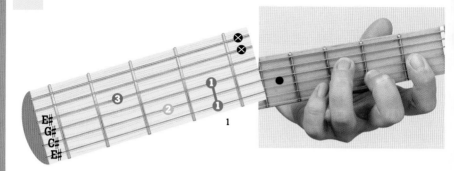

1 C♯/D♭ minor

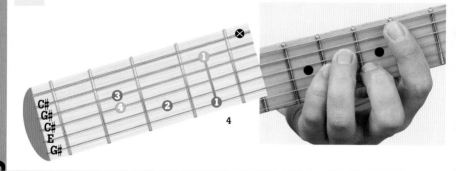

1 C♯7/D♭7

2   C♯/D♭ major

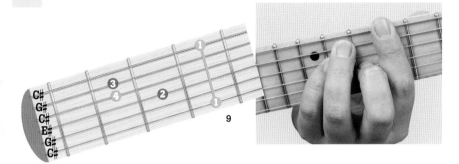

C♯
G♯
C♯
E♯
G♯
C♯

9

2   C♯/D♭ minor

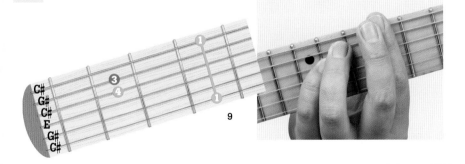

C♯
G♯
C♯
E
G♯
C♯

9

2   C♯7/D♭7

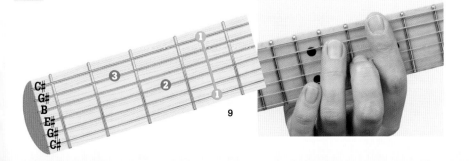

C♯
G♯
B
E♯
G♯
C♯

9

D

1 D major

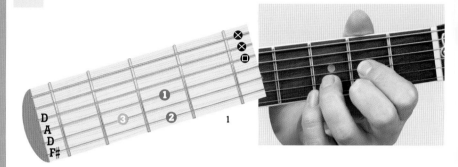

D
A
D
F#

1

1 D minor

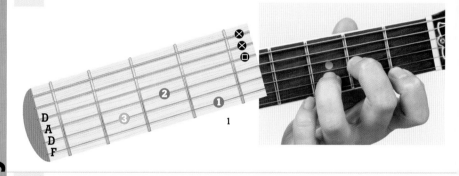

D
A
D
F

1

1 D7

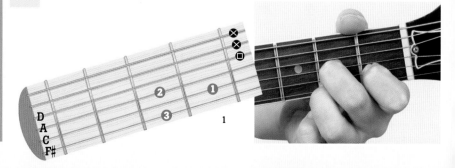

D
A
C
F#

1

2   D major

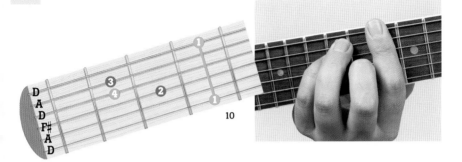

2   D minor

2   D7

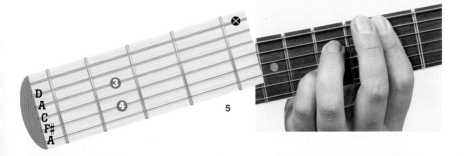

E♭/D♯

1 E♭/D♯ major

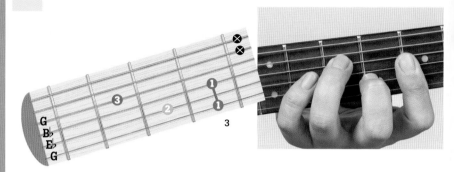

G
B♭
B♭
E♭
G

3

1 E♭/D♯ minor

E♭
B♭
E♭
G♭

1

1 E♭7/D♯7

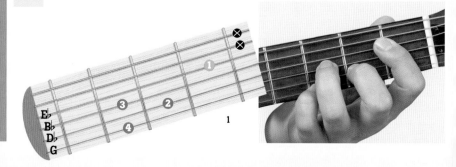

E♭
B♭
D♭
G

1

2 E♭/D♯ major

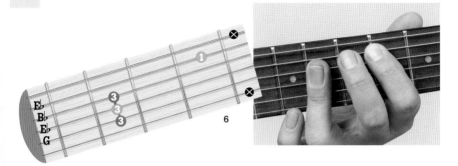

6

2 E♭/D♯ minor

6

2 E♭7/D♯7

6

E

1   E major

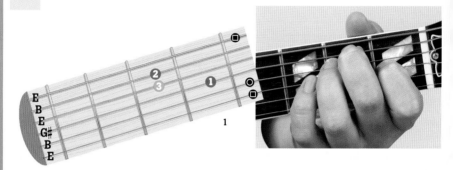

1   E minor

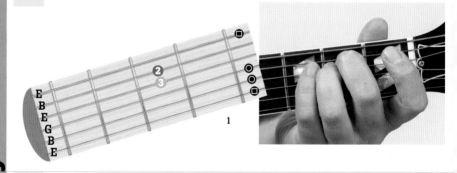

1   E7

2 E major

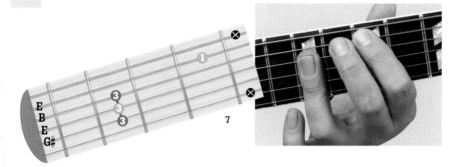

2 E minor

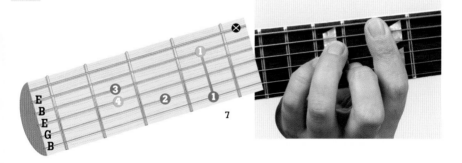

2 E7

F

1   F major

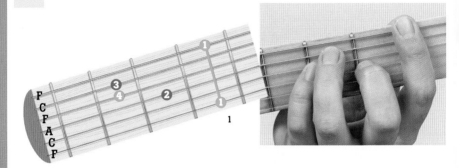

1   F minor

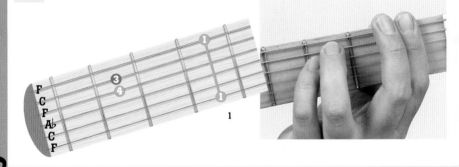

1   F7

2 F major

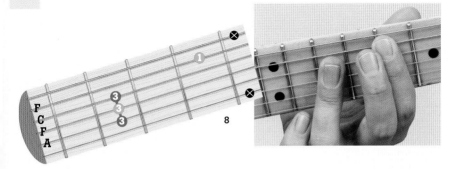

2 F minor

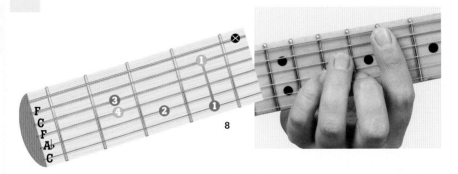

2 F7

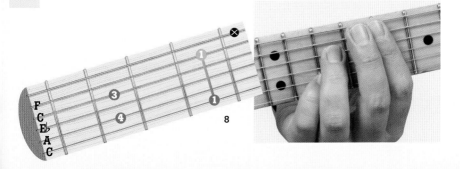

F♯/G♭

1 F♯/G♭ major

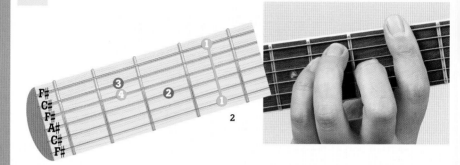

1 F♯/G♭ minor

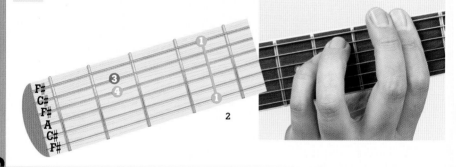

1 F♯7/G♭7

2 F♯/G♭ major

F♯
C♯
F♯
A♯

9

2 F♯/G♭ minor

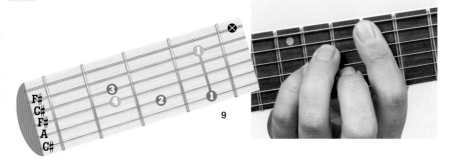

F♯
C♯
F♯
A
C♯

9

2 F♯7/G♭7

F♯
C♯
E
A♯
C♯

9

G

1 G major

1 G minor

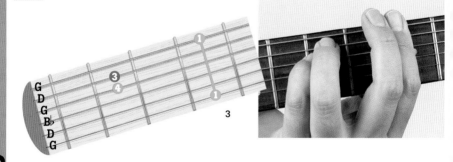

1 G7

2   G major

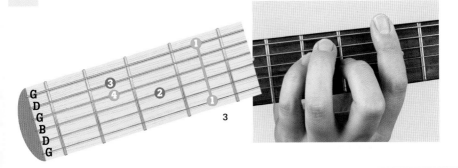

2   G minor

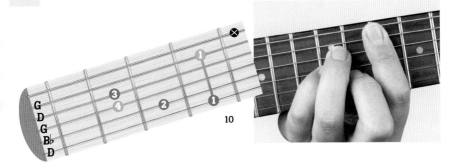

2   G7

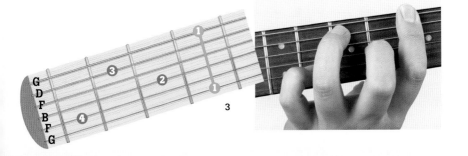

G♯/A♭

1   G♯/A♭ major

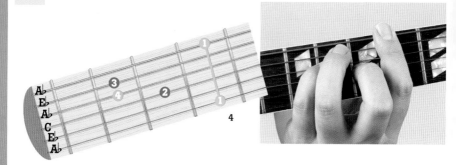

1   G♯/A♭ minor

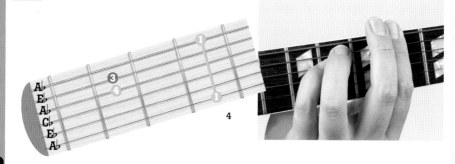

1   G♯7/A♭7

2   G#/A♭ major

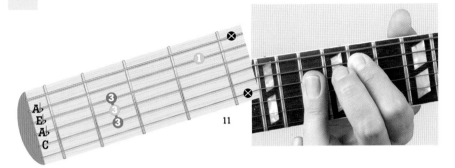

2   G#/A♭ minor

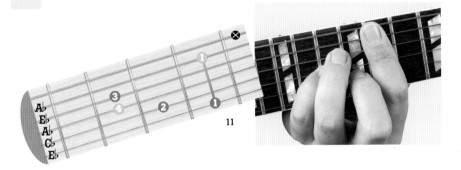

2   G#7/A♭7

A

1 A major

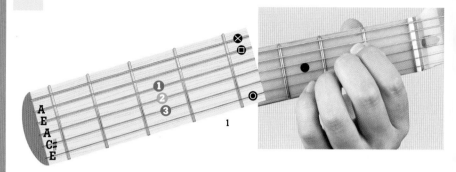

1 A minor

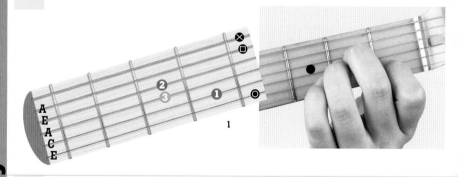

1 A7

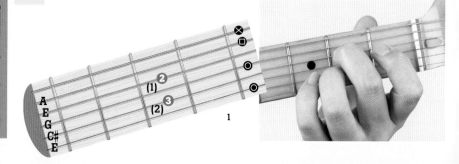

2 A major

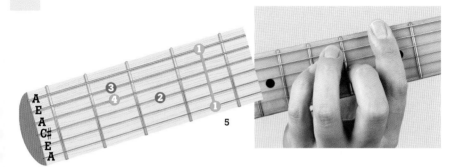

2 A minor

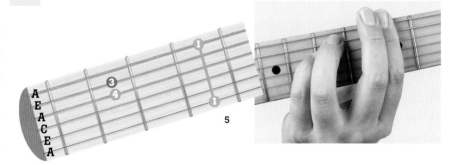

2 A7

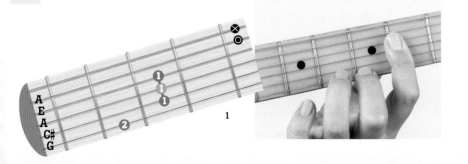

A♯/B♭

1 A♯/B♭ major

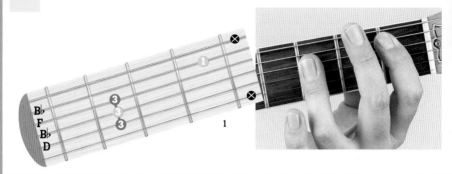

B♭
F
B♭
D

1

1 A♯/B♭ minor

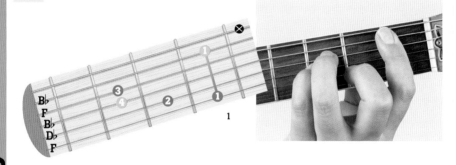

B♭
F
B♭
D♭
F

1

1 A♯7/B♭7

B♭
F
A♭
D
F

1

2 A♯/B♭ major

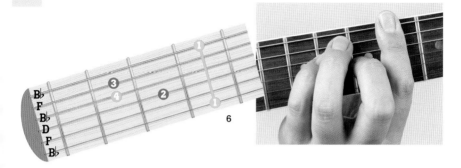

2 A♯/B♭ minor

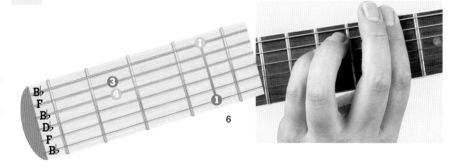

2 A♯7/B♭7

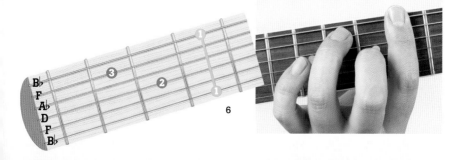

B

1 B major

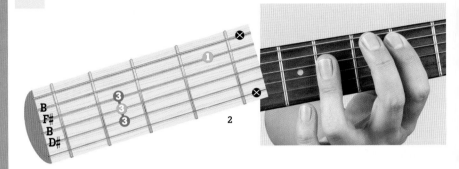

1 B minor

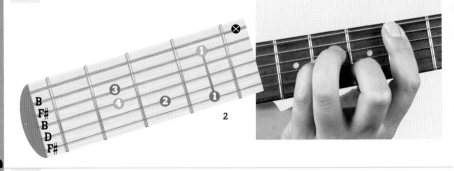

1 B7

Chord library

2   B major

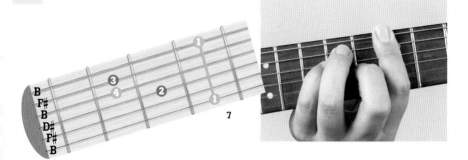

2   B minor

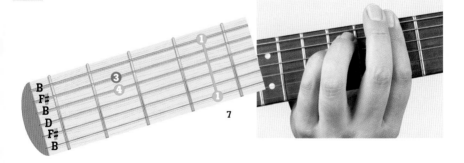

2   B7

Additional chords

Esus4

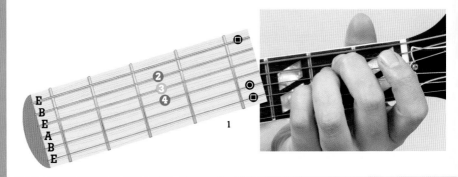

Asus4

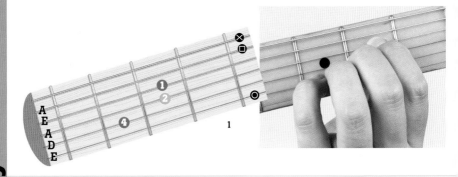

Dsus4

Emin7

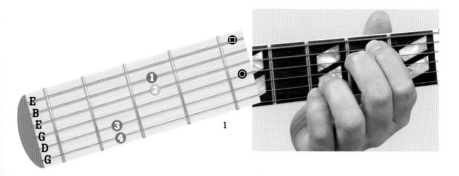

Amin7

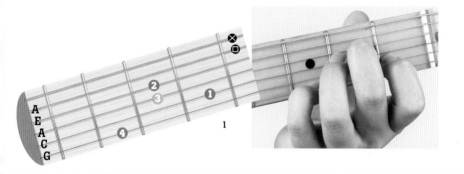

Dmin7

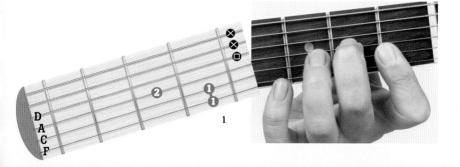

Scale library

C major

Shape 1

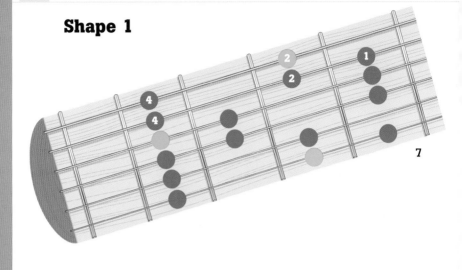

7

Shape 4

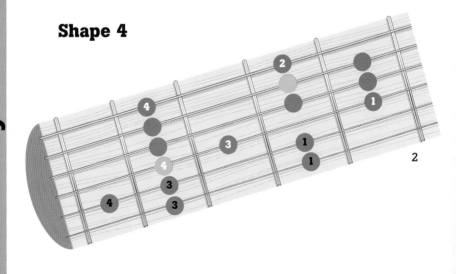

2

C natural minor

Shape 1

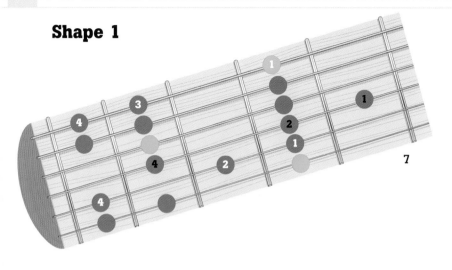

7

Shape 4

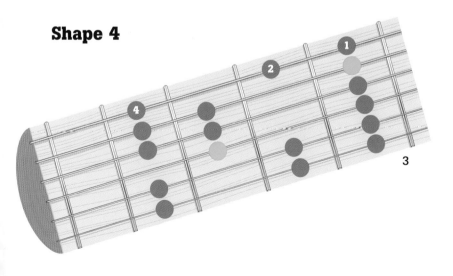

3

C minor pentatonic

Shape 1

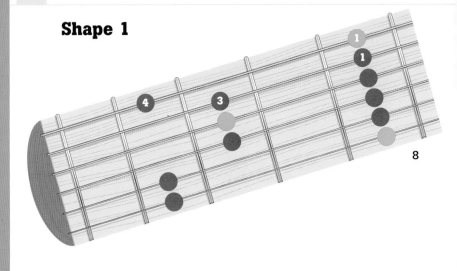

8

Shape 4

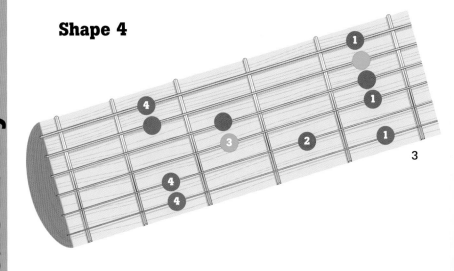

3

C blues scale

Shape 1

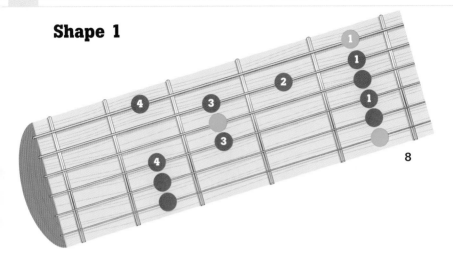

8

Shape 4

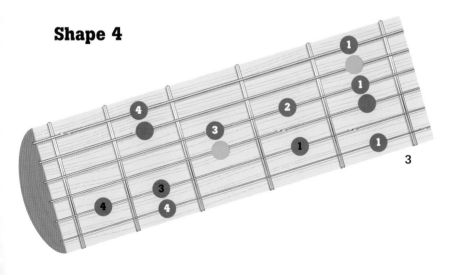

3

C#/Db major

Shape 1

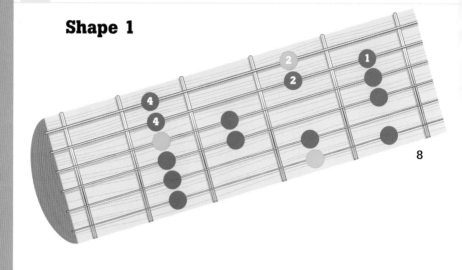

8

Shape 4

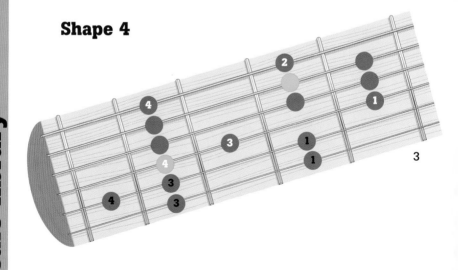

3

C♯/D♭ natural minor

Shape 1

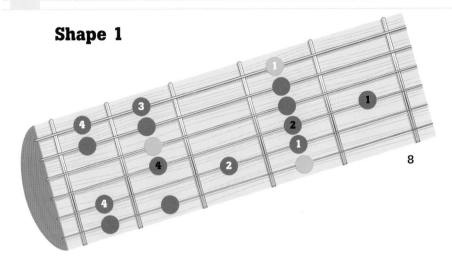

8

Shape 4

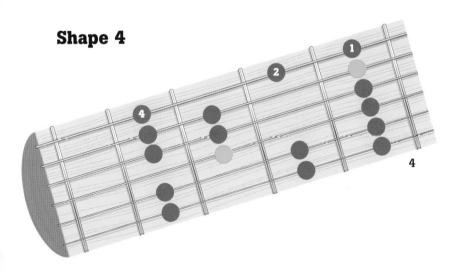

4

C#/D♭ minor pentatonic

Shape 1

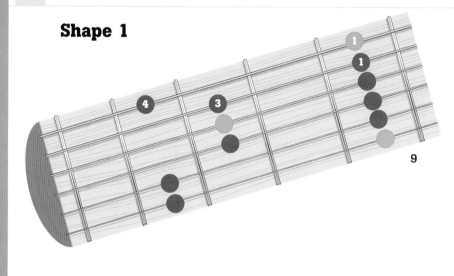

9

Shape 4

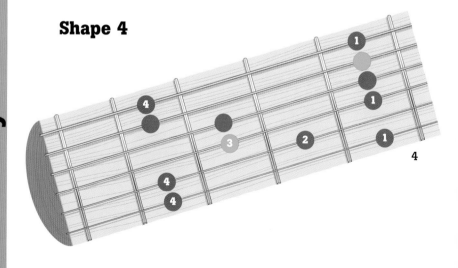

4

C#/Db blues scale

Shape 1

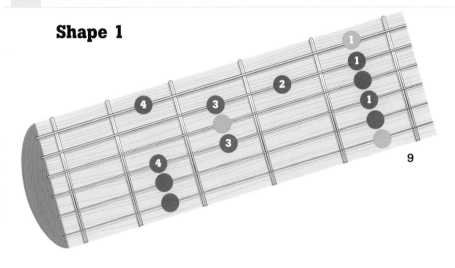

9

Shape 4

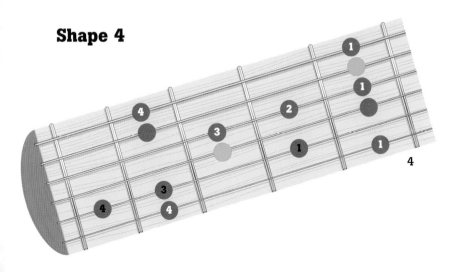

4

D major

Shape 1

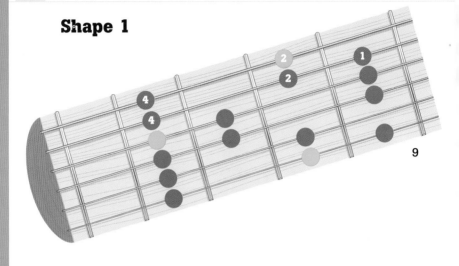

9

Shape 4

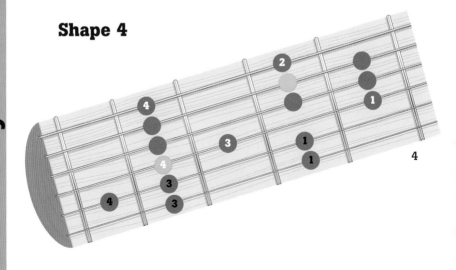

4

D natural minor

Shape 1

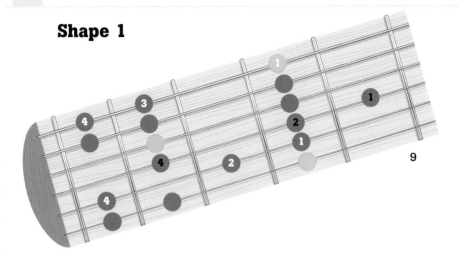

9

Shape 4

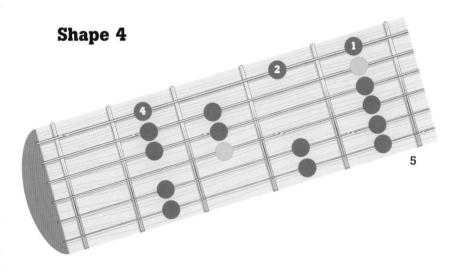

5

D minor pentatonic

Shape 1

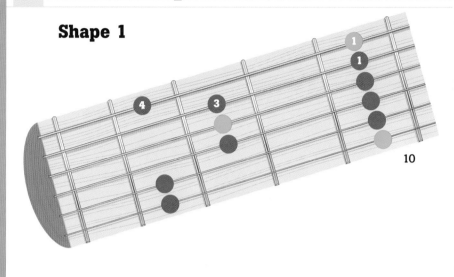

10

Shape 4

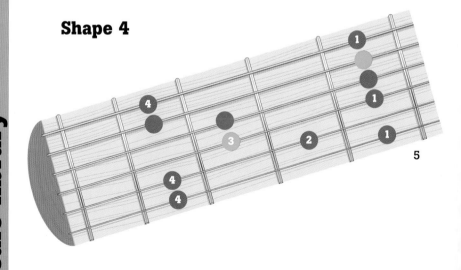

5

D blues scale

Shape 1

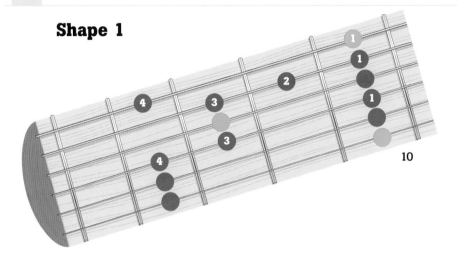

10

Shape 4

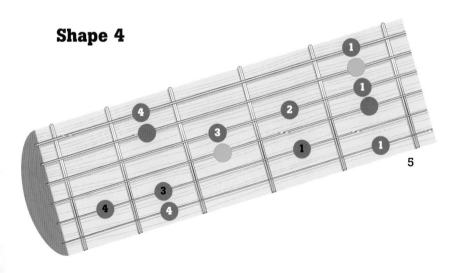

5

D♯/E♭ major

Shape 1

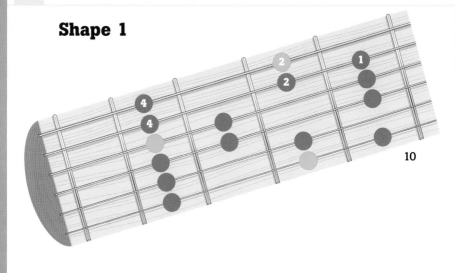

10

Shape 4

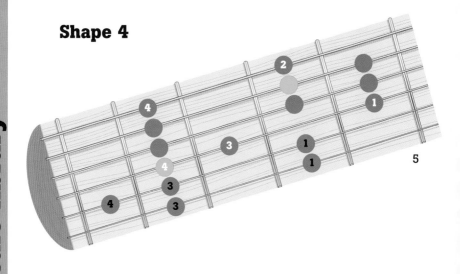

5

D#/E♭ natural minor

Shape 1

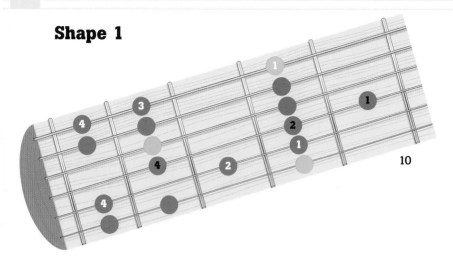

10

Shape 4

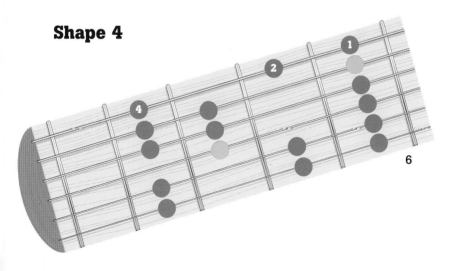

6

D♯/E♭ minor pentatonic

Shape 1

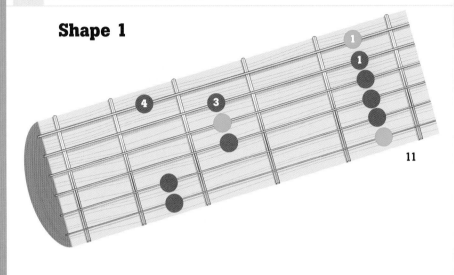

11

Shape 4

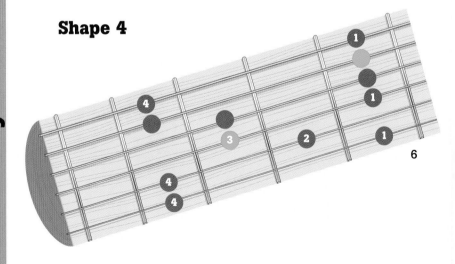

6

D#/E♭ blues scale

Shape 1

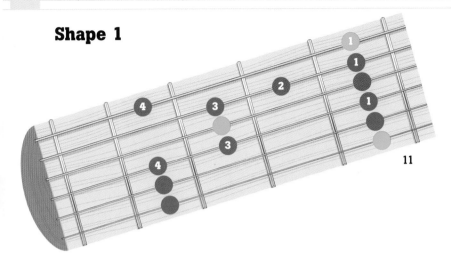

11

Shape 4

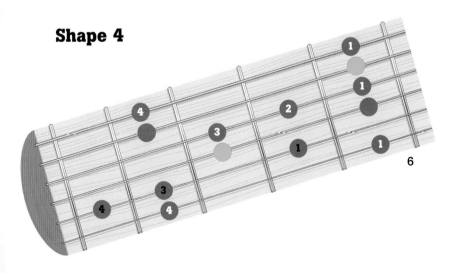

6

E major

Shape 1

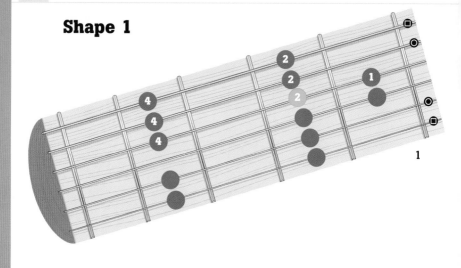

1

Shape 4

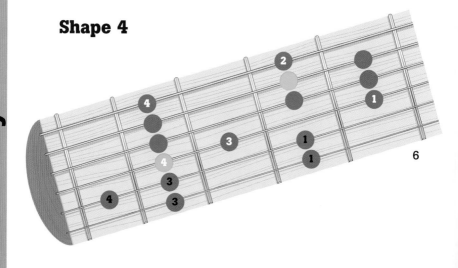

6

E natural minor

Shape 1

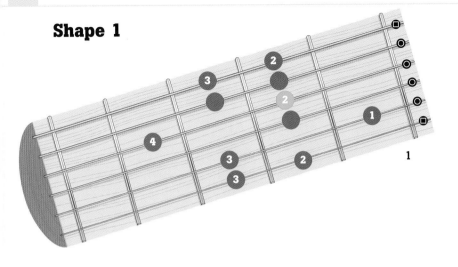

1

Shape 4

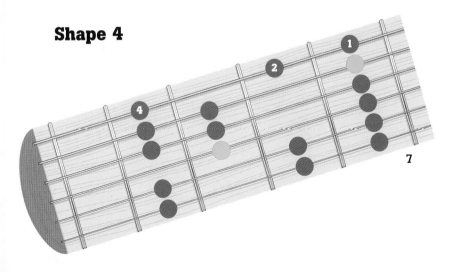

7

E minor pentatonic

Shape 1

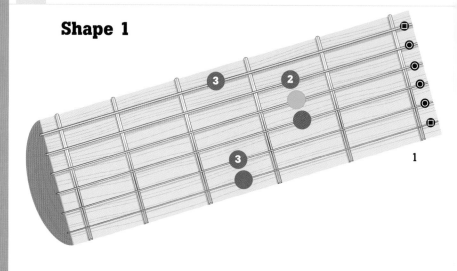

Shape 4

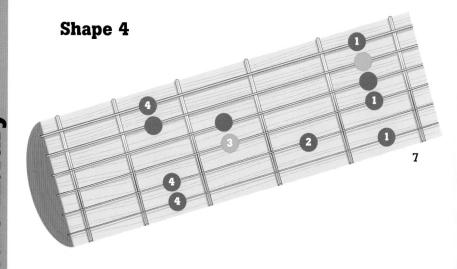

E blues scale

Shape 1

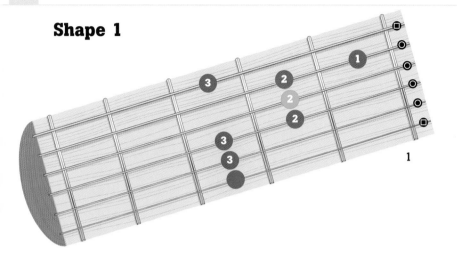

1

Shape 4

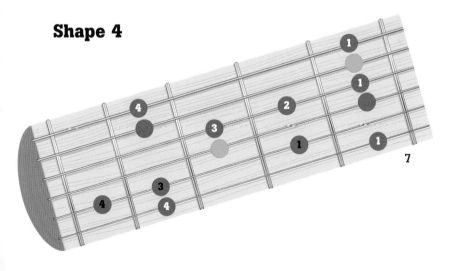

7

F major

Shape 1

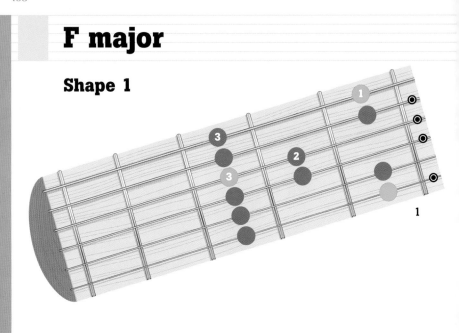

1

Shape 4

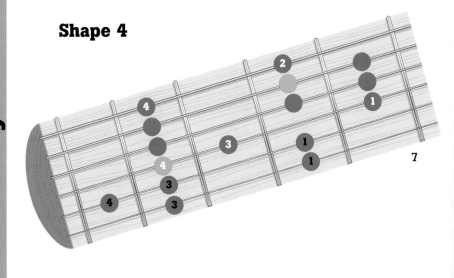

7

F natural minor

Shape 1

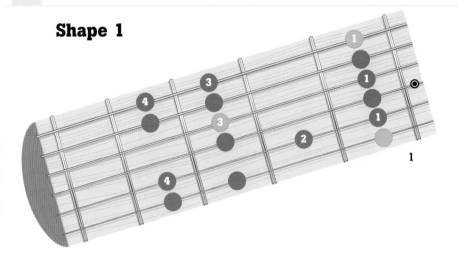

1

Shape 4

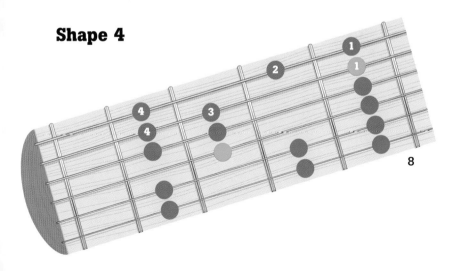

8

F minor pentatonic

Shape 1

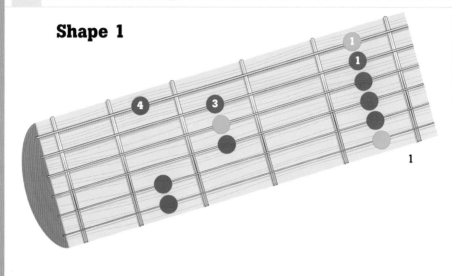

1

Shape 4

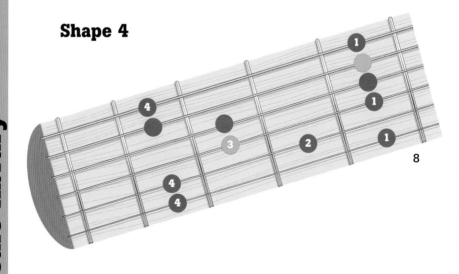

8

F blues scale

Shape 1

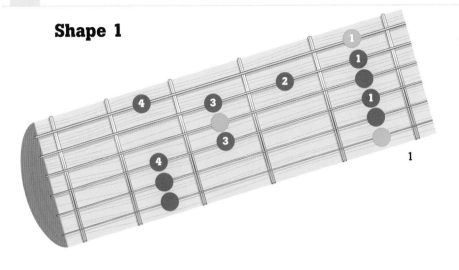

1

Shape 4

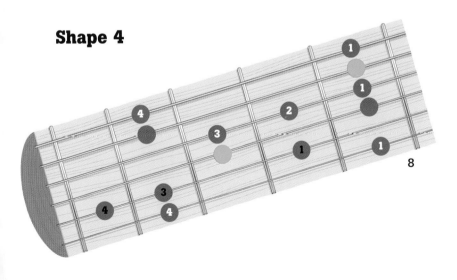

8

F♯/G♭ major

Shape 1

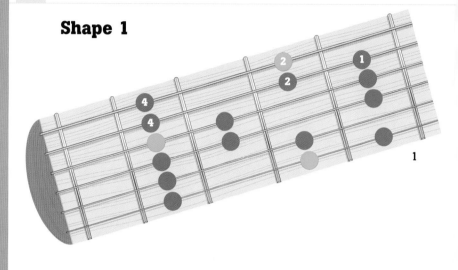

1

Shape 4

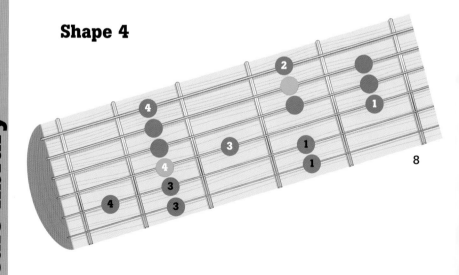

8

F#/G♭ natural minor

Shape 1

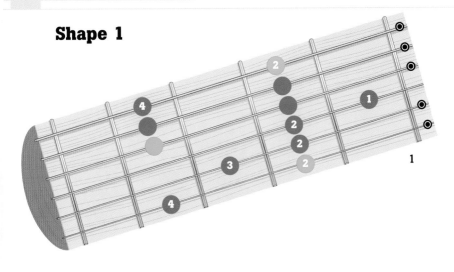

1

Shape 4

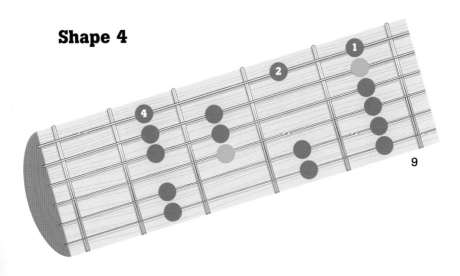

9

F♯/G♭ minor pentatonic

Shape 1

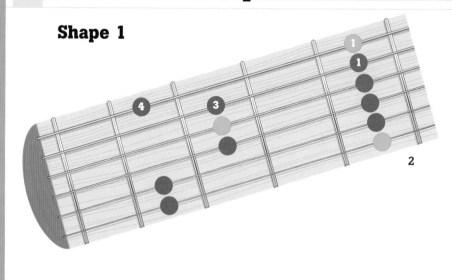

2

Shape 4

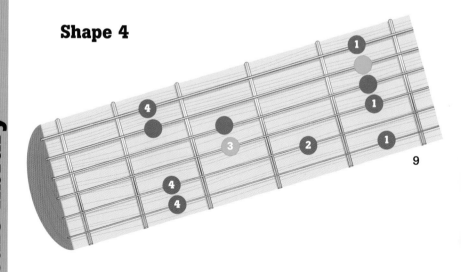

9

F#/G♭ blues scale

Shape 1

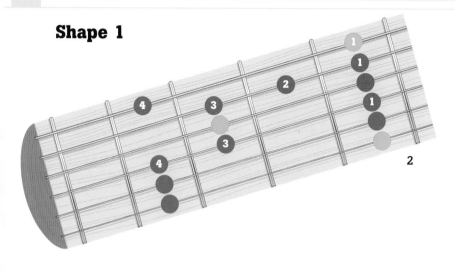

2

Shape 4

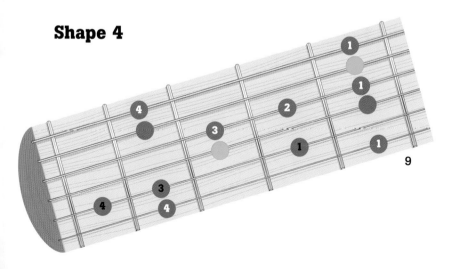

9

G major

Shape 1

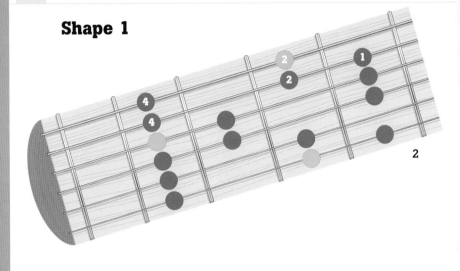

2

Shape 4

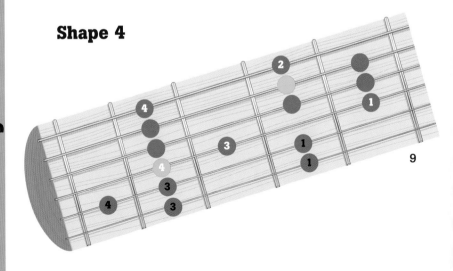

9

G natural minor

Shape 1

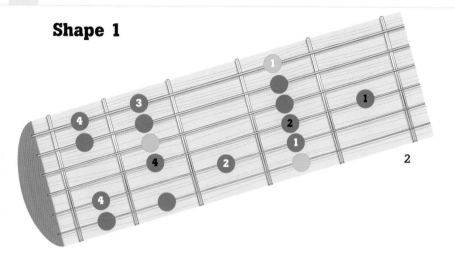

2

Shape 4

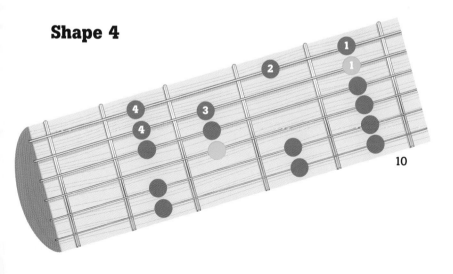

10

G minor pentatonic

Shape 1

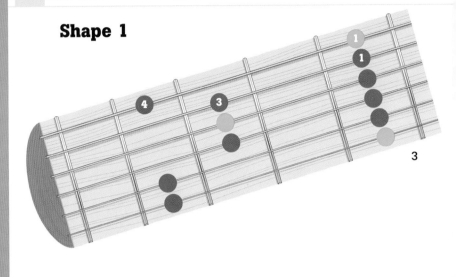

3

Shape 4

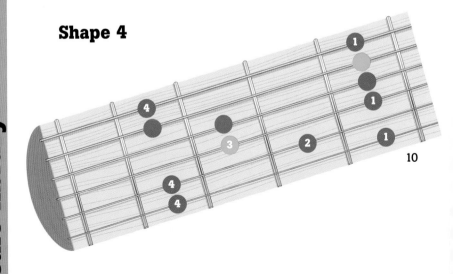

10

G blues scale

Shape 1

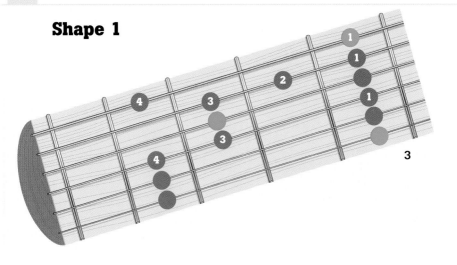

3

Shape 4

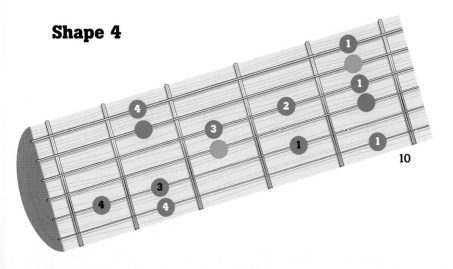

10

G♯A♭ major

Shape 1

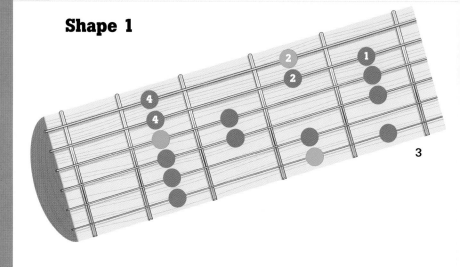

3

Shape 4

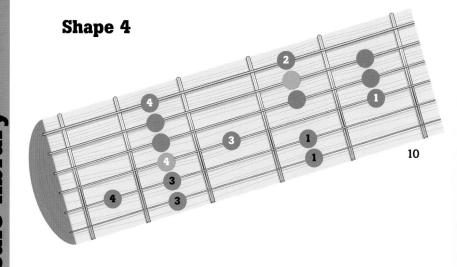

10

G♯A♭ natural minor

Shape 1

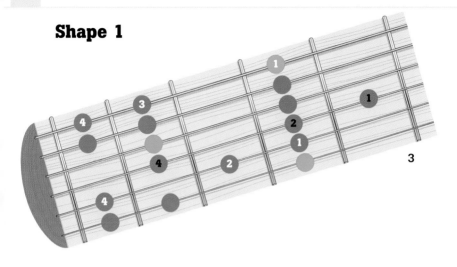

3

Shape 4

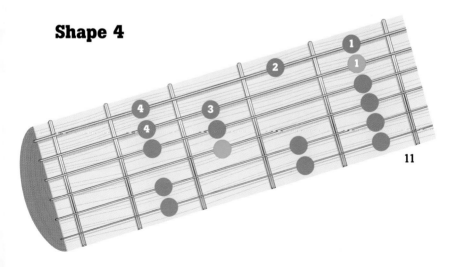

11

G♯/A♭ minor pentatonic

Shape 1

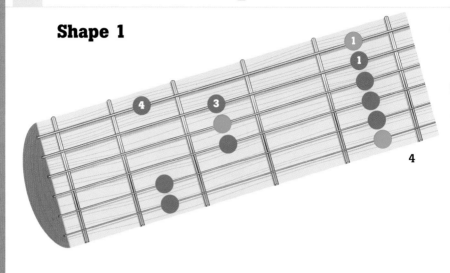

4

Shape 4

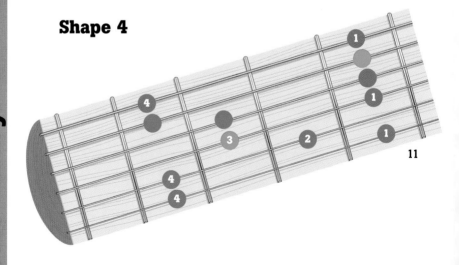

11

G#/A♭ blues scale

Shape 1

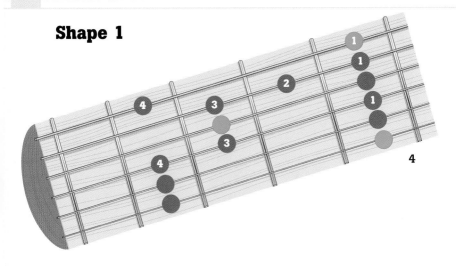

4

Shape 4

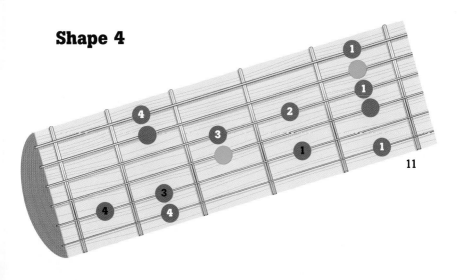

11

A major

Shape 1

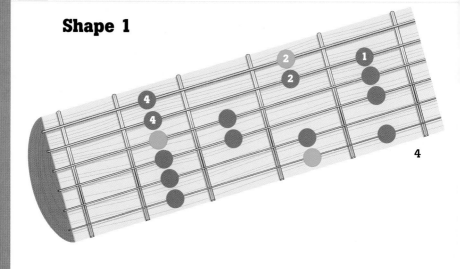

4

Shape 4

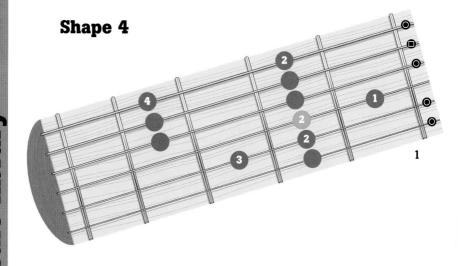

1

A natural minor

Shape 1

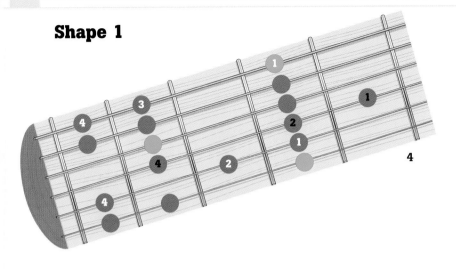

Shape 4

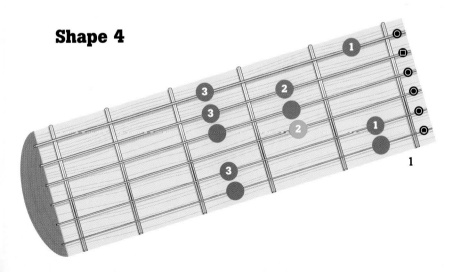

A minor pentatonic

Shape 1

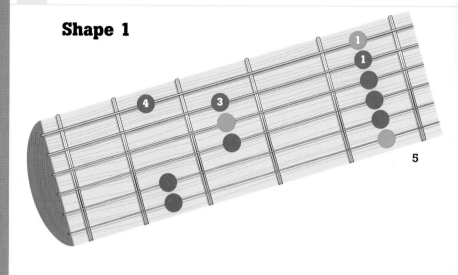

5

Shape 4

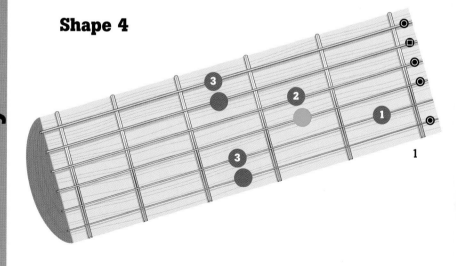

1

A blues scale

Shape 1

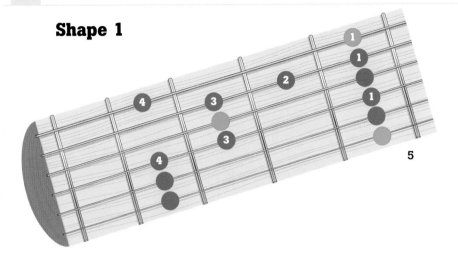

5

Shape 4

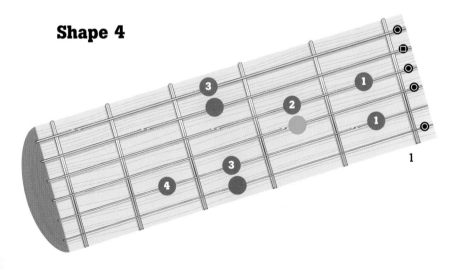

1

A♯/B♭ major

Shape 1

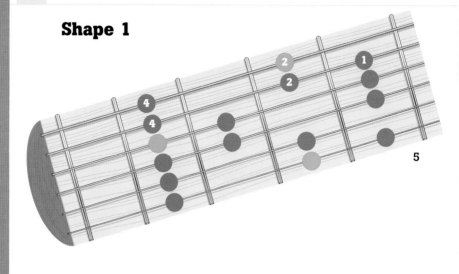

5

Shape 4

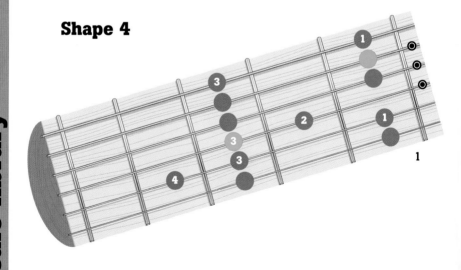

1

A#/B♭ natural minor

Shape 1

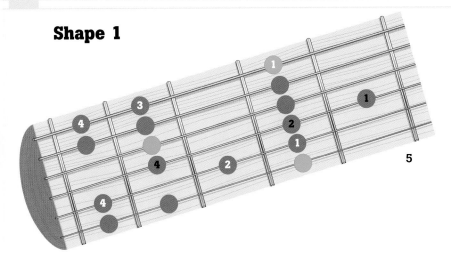

5

Shape 4

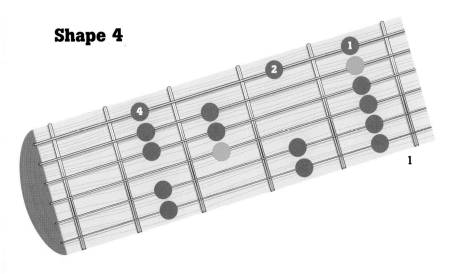

1

A#/B♭ minor pentatonic

Shape 1

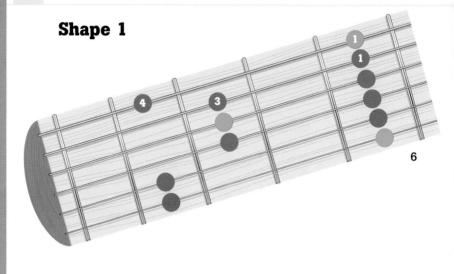

Shape 4

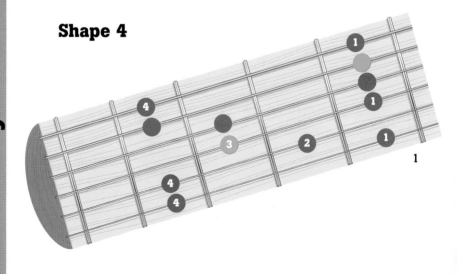

A#/B♭ blues scale

Shape 1

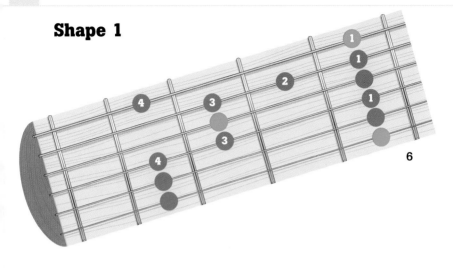

6

Shape 4

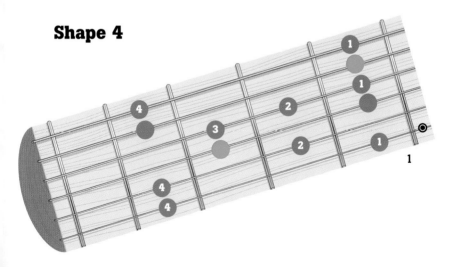

1

B major

Shape 1

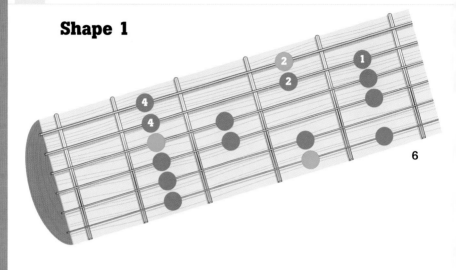

6

Shape 4

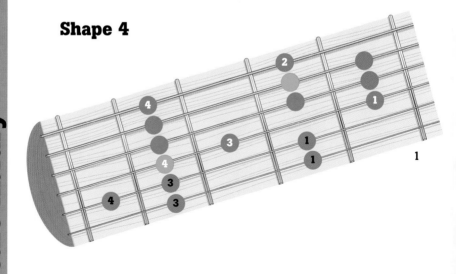

1

B natural minor

Shape 1

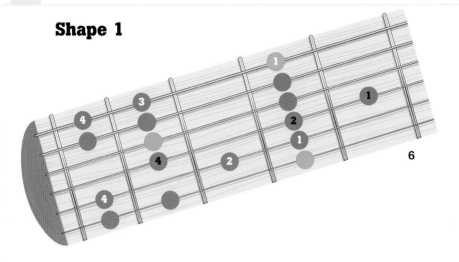

6

Shape 4

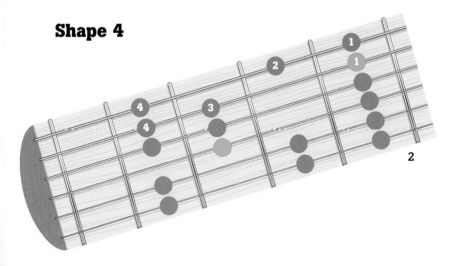

2

B minor pentatonic

Shape 1

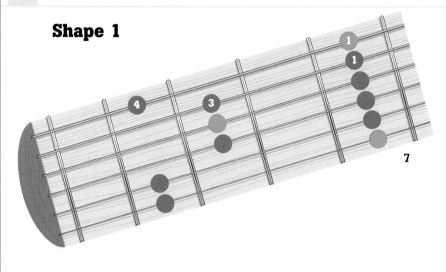

7

Shape 4

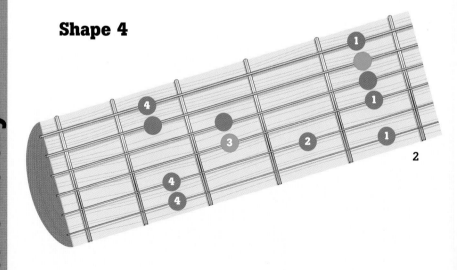

2

B blues scale

Shape 1

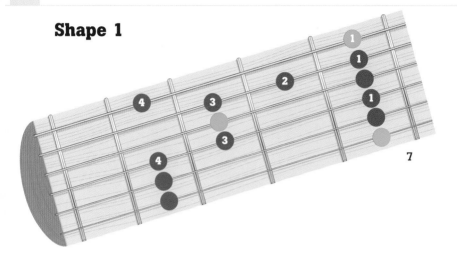

7

Shape 4

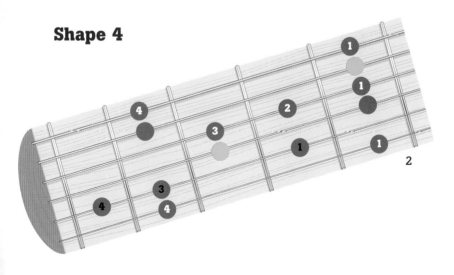

2

Buyer's guide

Fender Telecaster

The Telecaster was the first solid-bodied, electric guitar. It went on sale in 1950 under the name Broadcaster. However, this was swiftly changed to Telecaster in 1951, a preferable alternative since it sounded similar to "television" and therefore suggested cutting-edge technology. Amazingly, it has been in continuous production in various forms ever since.

Design
The Tele is the simplest of all electric guitar designs and features a one-piece body, bolt-on neck, two pick-ups (controlled by a three-position selector), one volume and one tone control.

Fans
This simplistic instrument has won the hearts of many players, most famously James Burton (Elvis Presley), Jimmy Page (the famous *Stairway to Heaven* solo was recorded on a Telecaster), Keith Richards, Joe Strummer, Frank Black (the Pixies), and jazz guitarists such as Mike Stern.

Price range
Fender currently offers a huge choice of models, ranging from the budget Squier to the fiercely expensive Custom Shop line. The Squier Tele is an ideal beginner's model and the cheapest option. More expensive, but offering excellent value, are the "made in Mexico" Standard Teles. These use cheaper parts than USA models, but are significantly better than the Squiers. Finally, the American Series Fender guitars are the "made in the USA" real deal, but you pay more for the privilege.

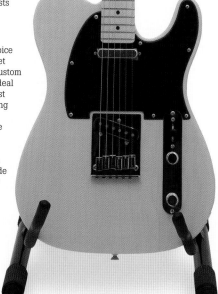

Fender Telecaster
US series
Blonde

Other manufacturers also make Tele-inspired guitars; the best of these is the Yamaha Pacifica (120SJ model), a well-made instrument that offers great value for money if you're not too bothered about owning the "real thing."

Secondhand Fender guitars are only a cheap option if they have been produced in the last 15 years or less. Earlier models start to rise in value sharply, with 1970s Fenders now commanding high prices—original 1950s models (even in poor condition) are now way out of the reach of the pocket of the average musician.

**Squier
Telecaster**
Metallic blue

**Fender
Telecaster**
*Mexican standard
Sunburst*

Fender Stratocaster

Undeniably the most iconic of all guitar designs, the Stratocaster has remained virtually unchanged since it was first introduced in 1954. The Strat looks as cool as it did during the birth of rock 'n' roll, and, despite fierce competition, it remains one of the world's top-selling guitars to this day.

Design

Like the Telecaster (see page 228), the Strat is based on a simple bolt-on neck design, but, unlike the Tele, the back of the body features a contoured design for increased comfort when playing. It also boasts three single coil pick-ups capable of providing a wide spectrum of tones that range from shimmering, glassy rhythm, through to fat, soaring lead, making the Strat an extremely versatile instrument.

Fans

The long list of legendary players of this instrument includes Jimi Hendrix, Eric Clapton, Jeff Beck, Dave Gilmour, and Mark Knopfler.

Price range

Fender now produces a huge range of these instruments. The basic three-tier price hierarchy starts with the Squier, moves up to the Mexican models (the "Standard" Strat), and culminates in the USA-built American Series.

Strat-style guitars are also available from other manufacturers; the best of these is the Yamaha Pacifica (012 and 112 models). Ibanez also produces a range of excellent "Strats," with the SAS36 model offering excellent value for money.

Fender Stratocaster
US series
Shoreline gold

Buyer's guide **Ten guitars**

The Stratocaster offers
the widest range of
sounds of any electric
guitar, but with so
many different models
and price ranges on offer,
it can be the most
bewildering guitar to buy.
So try as many different
kinds of instrument as
possible before you buy,
which will ensure you
find the one that's right
for you.

Fender
Stratocaster
Mexican standard
Electro blue

Squier
Stratocaster
Metallic red

Gibson Les Paul

Gibson's Les Paul model is one of the most recognizable solid-body electric guitars, its characteristic single-cutaway design remaining virtually unchanged for over half a century.

Design

With a thicker body design, the Les Paul is a heavier instrument than the Strat (see page 230) and this, when combined with the two double humbucker pick-ups fitted to the standard and custom models, gives this instrument a thick, distinctive tone with lots of sustain (as described by Nigel Tufnel of Spinal Tap, "it's famous for it's sustain, waaaaaaaah, you can go and have a bite, waaaaaaaah, and you'll still be hearing that one!").

Fans

Many pioneering players, including Jimmy Page, Peter Green, Gary More, Paul Kossoff, Slash, and Al DiMeola, have remained loyal to the Les Paul throughout their careers.

Price range

Gibson also offers budget versions of its top-selling models. These are manufactured in the Far East under the brand name Epiphone. The Epiphone Les Paul offers excellent value for money, costing a fraction of the price for a USA-built Gibson Les Paul Standard. Gibson doesn't make a mid-budget model such as Fender's Mexican Standard Series.

For non-Gibson alternatives, it's worth checking out the wide range of Les Paul-style guitars by ESP, Godin, and Gretsch.

Gibson Les Paul
Iced tea

Gibson SG

The SG (imaginatively, an abbreviation of "solid guitar") was Gibson's attempt to usurp the Fender Strat from the top-selling slot in the early 1960s. A major drawback of the Les Paul model is the inaccessibility of the higher frets when compared to the Strat. It is also a very heavy guitar with a thick body.

Design
The SG was designed to offer a double-cutaway, thin-bodied guitar that would rival the Strat's supremacy. Unfortunately, it never sold in the quantities that Gibson had hoped for; nonetheless, it has sold steadily and remained in production since its introduction in 1961. The SG is a great raunchy guitar, ideal for playing straight ahead, no-frills rock 'n' roll.

Fans
Famous players include Angus Young (AC/DC), Toni Iommi (the Black Sabbath guitarist who "invented" heavy metal), Eric Clapton (during the Cream period), and Frank Zappa.

Price range
Due to the thin-bodied simple design, the SG is easy to manufacture and so is one of Gibson's cheapest electric guitars. If your budget won't stretch to a Gibson model, check out the Epiphone SG310 model—this is a fantastic value-for-money instrument featuring an alder body and mahogany neck for a very low price.

Gibson SG
Standard
Cherry

Gibson ES-175

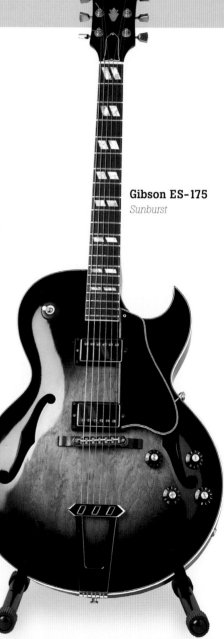

Gibson ES-175
Sunburst

The ES-175 was Gibson's first true electric guitar design and initially went on sale in 1949; next to the L5 it is probably the most famous jazz guitar in the world and is still in production today.

Design

Being hollow-bodied, this type of electric guitar is often described as being "semi-acoustic" since it can be played unamplified (albeit rather quietly). The ES prefix stands for "electric Spanish," although the instrument bears little resemblance to its Spanish cousin in sound or looks. The semi-acoustic design gives this instrument a warm, mellow tone and makes it an ideal choice for the jazz guitarist.

Fans

Many of the world's most famous jazzers have played an ES-175, with Wes Montgomery, Pat Metheny, Joe Pass, Pat Martino, and Herb Ellis heading a long list of legendary 175 disciples.

Price range

Hollow-bodied guitars are much more complex to manufacture than solid-bodied instruments, and this is reflected in the price. Although the ES-175 is Gibson's budget jazz guitar (it uses a plywood top instead of solid wood), it still retails higher than the top-of-the-range Les Paul Custom. However, Epiphone also produce a very reasonably priced ES-175 model that is well worth checking out.

Manufacturers such as ESP and Gretsch also make some fine semi-acoustic models, but top marks must go to Ibanez which produces a fantastic range of jazz semis, starting with the amazingly low-priced AF75 model.

Gibson ES-335

Although the ES-335 is labeled with Gibson's "electric Spanish" prefix, the 335 is, in fact, a hybrid design and was a radical departure from convention when it was first manufactured in 1958.

Design

The 335's body is very thin for a semi-acoustic instrument since it has a solid block of wood inside the guitar body underneath the pick-ups, which reduces the problem of feedback associated with semi-acoustic designs. The 335 offers the extra warmth and depth of tone associated with a full-bodied, semi-acoustic guitar, but with the versatility and high-volume capabilities of a solid-body design. This is a hugely versatile guitar capable of providing the full palette of sounds from warm and jazzy, bluesy tones to biting, soaring lead.

Fans

Famous 335 players span a wide range of styles from rock 'n' roll, blues and jazz fusion, and include Chuck Berry, George Harrison, BB King, Lee Ritenour, and Larry Carlton.

Price range

Slightly cheaper than the ES-175, the ES-335 is still an expensive purchase if you buy the original Gibson model. Opt for the many excellent Epiphone alternatives if you want one of these highly desirable instruments, but don't want to spend as much as it would cost to buy a reasonable secondhand car.

Washburn (HB32) and Yamaha (SA500) also produce some cool 335-style guitars, which are worthy of serious consideration if you're looking for a versatile semi-acoustic instrument.

Gibson ES-335
Flame maple

Parker Fly

There have been few departures from the traditional electric guitar designs that have proved popular or achieved sustained success. Parker Guitars are the exception to the rule. A relative newcomer to the guitar-manufacturing business, the company was started in the early 1990s by luthier Ken Parker. After spending many years building and repairing guitars, he began asking his customers what they most liked or disliked about their instruments. This provided him with the blueprint for the unusual-looking Parker Fly.

Design

The Parker Fly is characteristically a lightweight instrument, constructed from a combination of wood and composite materials. The original instruments featured a carbon-fiber fingerboard, which allowed an ultra-low action to be achieved, making the instrument extremely playable. Unusually, the guitar was also fitted with a piezo-bridge pick-up in addition to the two humbuckers; consequently, this instrument produces an incredible range of sounds and is possibly one of the most versatile electric guitars you can buy.

Fans

Famous endorsers of The Fly include Joe Walsh (The Eagles), Joni Mitchell, Larry Corryell, and a long list of eminent USA session guitarists.

Price range

Although the full-blown Parker Fly is an extremely expensive guitar, the company's range has expanded over the years to include more reasonably priced instruments. The P36 and P42 models are the company's entry-level models and offer excellent value for money. If you want to stand out from the crowd, add a Parker guitar to the top of your shopping list.

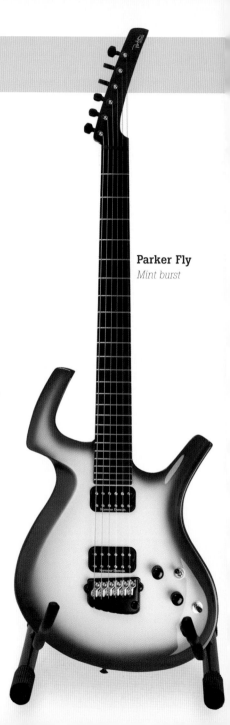

Parker Fly
Mint burst

Steel-string acoustic

The modern steel-string acoustic guitar (also known as a "flat-top" guitar) evolved from the early instruments produced by the C. F. Martin company in the mid-1800s. This famous American company still builds prestige acoustics to this day. The steel-string acoustic is probably everyone's idea of a first guitar. Unfortunately, the paradox is that budget models can actually be quite hard to play due to the combination of a high action and heavy steel strings. However, most guitar shops will offer a free "set-up" when you buy, so ask to have the action lowered and offer to pay for a new set of light-gauge strings to be fitted. The shop assistant will probably argue that you shouldn't put light-gauge strings on an acoustic, but there's no point in making the learning process harder than it needs to be. Smile knowingly and say that heavy-gauge strings are for the pros.

Yamaha DW7

Price range

If you want a playable instrument that will stay in tune, a reasonable steel-string instrument is not going to be much cheaper than an electric guitar. However, it will be more portable, more versatile (it can be played pick or fingerstyle), and a lot easier just to grab and play, which means you'll probably practice more.

The "pick of the best" budget steel-string acoustics include the Fender CD60 and CD100, Yamaha F310, and the Epiphone AJ100. These instruments are large-bodied "dreadnought"-style acoustics designed to produce a big sound. If you don't want a large-bodied guitar, choose a "parlor-size" or "folk-bodied" model. Well worth investigating are the Daisy Rock Pixie or the Yamaha FS720.

Classical guitar

The nylon-string classical guitar (also called a Spanish guitar) is the "oldest" of all the guitars here, and has a long and distinguished pedigree. The instrument evolved in Spain and has an impressive repertoire dating back to the early seventeenth century. The nylon-string guitar isn't just for classical music—it is also a favorite with folk and Latin guitarists; it can be strummed or fingerpicked just like a steel-string, but those low-tension nylon strings won't hurt your fingers. So, in some ways it is the ideal beginner's guitar. The good news is that a cheap nylon-strung guitar is much more playable than a cheap steel-string guitar; the bad news is that the fingerboard is wider, and even good instruments can slip out of tune quickly.

Price range

If you don't want to make a big financial commitment to learning the guitar straight away, then a classical acoustic is an ideal investment. Even if you move onto an electric or steel-string acoustic at a later date, a nylon-string guitar is a useful second guitar to have.

You can buy cheaper, but the Ibanez GA-5W is an excellent value-for-money instrument, which still retains good build quality. Equally good is the Yamaha C40 model. If you have a little more cash to spend, try the Tanglewood Concert Classic TC0 Guitar.

Admira Artista

Electro-acoustic

The electro-acoustic is not a hybrid
instrument capable of delivering
screaming lead one minute and gentle
fingerstyle accompaniment the next;
it's merely an acoustic that you can
plug into an amplifier—it still sounds
the same, only louder.

Design

These guitars look much the same as
a regular acoustic apart from the single
cutaway (offering easier access to
the higher frets) that has become
de rigueur on most models. They are
also fitted with a piezo-bridge pick-up,
a jack socket (usually discreetly
incorporated into the strap button),
and a volume and tone control. Some
models are also equipped with a small
5-band graphic equalizer. The
electronics are powered by a standard
9-volt battery; which is usually located
in a compartment next to the tone and
volume controls. One of the nicest
things about the electro-acoustic is
that it is often slightly smaller in size
with a shallower body. This is because
the instrument's acoustic volume is
no longer a primary consideration;
a large-bodied guitar would actually
be more prone to unpleasant feedback
when plugged in.

Price range

Because of the more complicated
cutaway design and added
electronics, these guitars are more
expensive than their acoustic
cousins. Yamaha has arguably
been a class leader in producing
keenly priced electro-acoustic
instruments for some time. The
APX500 is a very reasonably
priced instrument and should
be top of your shopping list if
you are in the market for an electro.
Runners-up include the Ibanez AEG-
8E, Ovation Applause AE-128, and
the Fender CD-60CE and CD-100CE.

Taylor 514CE

Ten essential accessories

Once you've bought your guitar, you will soon realize that an accessory or two will come in handy. To avoid wasting your hard-earned cash, the top ten of useful guitar accessories are listed below. Some of these are optional items, such as a strap; others, like the tuner, are simply indispensable. Now you will never need to receive a pair of socks as a present again—just drop a few hints to your family and friends when Christmas or a birthday is near!

Case

Most guitars these days come with a soft case that won't offer your guitar much protection. Lightweight fiberglass cases are the toughest, and essential if you intend taking your guitar on an airplane. Also well worth a look are the numerous types of "gig bags" that are now available. These allow you to carry your guitar on your back like a rucksack, making light work of traveling with your guitar.

Gig bag

Budget price range

Expensive price range

Mid-price range

Capo

These handy little devices are great for changing the key of an open-string picking pattern, and are used by acoustic and electric players alike. Well worth investing in if you intend accompanying yourself singing, a capo makes changing keys easy.

Fiberglass case

Strap

If you're keen to start gigging, then invest in a good-quality leather strap. A cheap strap will soon stretch and cannot be trusted to hang your prized possession from.

Spare strings

There's no doubt about it, you will definitely break a string at some time, and as there's nothing worse than not having a replacement to hand, you should invest in a spare set as soon as possible.

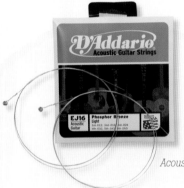

Electric guitar strings

Acoustic guitar strings

Lead

Obviously, this will not be very useful if you're strictly an acoustic player. However, if you've just bought an electric guitar "starter pack," then throw away the low-quality bundled lead and go for something better. Although a good-quality lead isn't cheap, the signal quality is far superior and it should last for years.

Music stand

Once you've bought one of these, you'll wonder why you spent so long propping your music up against the arm of the couch. Opt for a collapsible metal type that can be easily packed away for travel.

Guitar care

At the very least, you will need a cloth to wipe your guitar strings when you've finished playing. This prolongs the life of the strings and prevents an unpleasant build-up of grime. There's a wide range of guitar-care products on the market— polish, fretboard cleaner, treatments to prolong string life, cleaning cloths, peg winders (to make light work of string changing)—all of which are designed to help you keep your guitar in tip-top condition.

Peg winders

Metronome

This is not the most exciting purchase you could make, but is definitely one of the wisest. By practicing with a metronome on a regular basis, your sense of rhythm will soon be keenly honed.

Digital metronome

Modern metronome

Traditional metronome

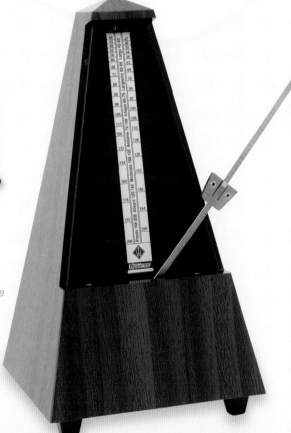

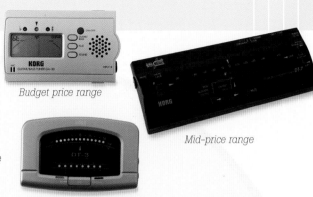

Guitar tuner

These handy little devices are an absolutely must-have. If you only buy one thing from this list, make sure it's one of these. Most tuners are automatic these days, so all you have to do is plug in and tune up. Prices have fallen considerably in recent years with the influx of goods manufactured in the Far East, so you won't find it too expensive to buy.

Budget price range

Mid-price range

Expensive price range

Guitar stand

Keeping your guitar on a stand, instead of tucked away under the bed in its case, makes it easier to practice frequently. You can just grab your instrument and start playing—you'll wonder why you never bought one of these sooner.

*"A" frame
guitar stand*

Traditional guitar stand

Choosing amps

An amplifier, or "amp," can transform an electric guitar's feeble unamplified sound into an earth-shattering roar. But even more importantly, it defines the tone and texture of its sound.

When the first electric guitars were produced, valve technology was king, so all early amps were valve based. This technology has stuck because a valve amp sounds warmer and more musical. It will respond to a pick in a way that a "solid-state" (i.e. non-valve) amplifier cannot. It is also more responsive to the guitar's volume control.

You don't need to spend a fortune, however, to be the lucky owner of an original valve amp from the 1970s or even the late 60s. Although prices are rising fast, they have not caught up with the value of guitars from this era—you can still find second-hand bargains. (If you buy privately, be sure to get your amp checked out by a qualified engineer as they produce potentially lethal voltages.)

While the USA has consistently dominated the guitar market, the amp market is not so clearly defined. Fender traditionally produces "cleaner" sounding amps that are more suited to jazz, blues, and country. However, in the 60s, two important British companies emerged: Vox (made famous by The Beatles who used Vox exclusively), and Marshall (famously endorsed by Jimi Hendrix, Jimmy Page, and many others). All three of these companies now produce valve and solid-state amplifiers. There are also many "boutique" companies that build expensive hand-wired valve amps that remain true to the original designs of the 50s.

The stack

The Marshall stack is one of those evocative images associated with the electric guitar. Jimi Hendrix playing with his teeth, Ritchie Blackmore launching into the intro of Smoke on the Water, Billie Joe Armstrong blasting out a punk rock anthem—these are defining moments of rock 'n' roll and all of them were performed in front of a wall of Marshall stacks. However, cool they may be, but unless you've got money to burn and your own personal roadie, they are not a practical option.

The combo

Combo amplifiers first emerged in the 1950s. They are smaller than the "stack" since the amp and speaker(s) are combined into a single cabinet. All the major manufacturers make a huge range of combo amps from small practice amps to back-breaking 100-watt monsters. If you're hankering after a valve practice amp, you owe it to yourself to check out the Epiphone Valve Junior. This amp is great value and, although it's rated at just 15 watts, it's LOUD!

Amp modeling/computer software

Over the last decade, computer-based amp-modeling software (such as the excellent "Guitar Rig" by Native Instruments) has become extremely popular. Alternatively, self-contained guitar processing units (these have no speakers and need to be plugged into an external amplifier) like the superb POD XT by Line 6, do not need a host computer. Both types of device are designed for recording; there is no need to upset the neighbors by "cranking up" an amp to get a good sound. However, most guitarists steer clear of guitar processors when playing live as they are just too fiddly.

The headphone amp

There are some excellent headphone amplifiers on the market today. These pocket-sized gadgets manage to pack in a very usable set of amp-modeled sounds, a drum machine, tuner, and even a time-stretching facility for slowing down those "hard-to-nail" licks! If you want to practice in complete privacy without disturbing anyone, these little gadgets are well worth a look. Korg's brilliant Pandora series offers particularly good value for money and includes all the above features.

Picks

Unless you choose to play entirely fingerstyle, the pick, or plectrum, will be your principle tool for getting sound out of your instrument. This small, triangular shape with rounded edges (traditionally made from tortoiseshell but now made from plastic) comes in many different shapes and sizes. Choosing the right pick is crucial to getting a good sound from your instrument—thicker picks are harder to use, but result in a "bigger" tone; thinner picks are easier to use, but result in a less "rounded" tone. Most guitarists opt for the middle ground and flexibility of medium-gauge picks (picks are frequently graded as thin, medium, or heavy, although many manufacturers offer a wider range of thicknesses ranging from 0.38mm to 1.5mm). However, not all guitarists use standard picks—many legendary players swear by unorthodox shapes and materials (felt, metal, and stone are not uncommon); Brian May (of Queen) swears by an English silver sixpenny piece! Listed below are a few of the most common types available. If you're not sure which one to start with, you can't go wrong with the workhorse of picks: a standard medium-gauge plastic pick.

Holding the pick

The pick should be grasped firmly between your first finger and thumb, with the thinnest end pointing in toward the guitar strings. Start by using downstrokes only—i.e. picking down toward your feet. Many guitarists also use their third and/or fourth finger to "anchor" their picking hand on the pick-guard or guitar body; in this way, the picking hand remains steady and there is no need to keep continually looking at it (something you should always avoid so you don't develop a bad habit).

Standard plastic pick

Available in a wide range of thicknesses to suit all styles and the best starting point for the beginner. Many are available with a high-grip surface at the base of the pick.

Teardrop pick

These picks are smaller in size than the standard pick so can be tricky to use; thicker gauges are a favorite with jazz guitarists.

Stainless steel pick

Popular with rock "metal" guitarists, this pick is chosen for its brash sound and attack. Beware, however, that they can shorten string life and even damage the finish of your guitar.

The "sharkfin" pick

The "sharkfin" is so called because of its unusual shape—many guitarists favor this radical and striking design. Both the smooth and serrated edge of the pick can be used to strike the strings.

Equal-sided pick

Available in a range of sizes and thicknesses, many guitarists favor this type of pick since any corner can be used to hit the strings.

Tricks of the trade

Remember to "anchor" your picking hand by gently resting your third and/or fourth finger on the guitar or pick-guard. This will prevent your pick from wandering away from the strings.

Emergency picks

Below are three templates that you can use to fashion your own picks. Cut the templates out and then draw around them on the material of your choice to provide a cutting line. In an emergency, you could always grab your credit card (the perfect material and thickness) and get cutting!

Glossary of terms

arpeggios An arpeggio is the notes of a chord played individually as opposed to being sounded simultaneously. They are an invaluable tool for creating melodies and improvisations.

back beat A term used to describe the emphasis of the weak beats two and four (in 4/4 time) in popular music. This is usually emphasised by the drummer (and played on the snare drum) but is also reinforced by the rhythm guitarist.

barre chords By fretting across the strings with the first finger, and re-fingering an open chord shape in front of it, a moveable chord shape is then created. The most common barre chords are type one (based on an open E chord) and type two (based on an open A chord).

consonance An interval or chord is described as being "stable" when consonant. This is created by the series of harmonic overtones that are created when the notes are sounded simultaneously. A consonant chord or interval is used to release the tension created by dissonant chords and intervals.

damping When a string or strings are muted by releasing the pressure of the fretting hand, or by touching the strings with the palm of the picking hand near the bridge, the string(s) are said to be damped.

diatonic The term diatonic is applied to any note, interval, or chord that occurs naturally in a major or minor key (i.e. without requiring any scale note to be changed with a sharp, flat, or natural).

dissonance The opposite of consonance, a dissonant chord or interval is said to be unstable. Dissonance is used to create motion in harmony by creating a need for resolution. This is described as "tension and release"—the dissonance provides tension, which is released when consonance occurs.

dominant 7th chord A major chord (triad) with a fourth note added a minor third above the fifth. This creates a minor seventh interval from the chord's root note. The chord occurs diatonically on the fifth (V or dominant) degree of the major scale and resolves naturally to the scale's tonic (I) chord. It is described as a dissonant chord because of the diminished fifth interval between the major third and minor seventh.

fingerpicking The technique of plucking the strings with the fingers as opposed to using a pick or plectrum. This is a popular technique with solo guitarists since simultaneous melody and accompaniment can be played more easily.

ghosted strumming The practice of lifting the pick off the strings to maintain a constant alternate strumming pattern, thus avoiding hitting the chord on every down or up stroke. Keeping the strumming hand moving constantly up and down in this way creates a much stronger rhythm.

hammer-on A hammer-on is created when only the first of two notes on the same string is picked— the second is created by fretting the note sharply ("hammering" the finger onto the fingerboard) without picking it. If the first note is not an open string, it must be fretted throughout.

hybrid picking A technique first developed by country guitarist Merle Travis. It involves picking a higher string simultaneously with a note played with the pick (plectrum). This is best achieved with your second (m) or third (a) picking hand finger.

legato A term that literally means to play smoothly or "tied together." Guitarists achieve this by playing consecutive hammer-ons and pull-offs.

machine heads/tuning pegs These are the adjustable knobs located on the guitar's headstock and are used to tension the strings. There is one tuning peg for each string, enabling each string to be tuned individually.

major chord The major chord is the most consonant (i.e. stable) chord in music. It is a triad constructed from the first, third, and fifth degrees of the major scale. Often described as a "happy"-sounding chord.

minor chord The minor chord is slightly less consonant (i.e. stable) than a major chord due to the relationship between the root (lowest) note of the chord and the minor third. It is constructed from the first, third, and fifth degrees of the harmonic minor scale. Often described as a "sad"-sounding chord.

moveable chord A non-open chord that does not incorporate open strings and so can be played anywhere on the neck. Moveable chords are extremely useful since they allow the guitarist to play in any key.

off-beat When counting in common time (4/4), the off-beats occur naturally between each beat. Counting "+" between the main beats will make it easier to locate the off-beats more accurately. A single bar of 4/4 would then be counted as "1 + 2 + 3 + 4 +".

open chord A chord played in first position and using open strings. The five principle open chord shapes are C, A, G, E, and D. Generally speaking, open chords are non-moveable.

pick up These are situated under the strings on the body of an electric guitar, and "pick up" the vibrations of the strings. Electromagnetic devices that essentially functions as a simple microphone, they convert the vibrations of each string into an electric signal, which is then amplified by a guitar amplifier or "amp."

pinch The process of playing two notes simultaneously, usually by picking with the thumb and a finger. However, the same effect can also be achieved with hybrid picking.

positions (e.g. third position) The position of the left hand on the fingerboard. When playing in "first position," the first finger plays all notes on the first fret, the second finger all notes on the second fret, and so on. So for "third position" the hand moves up the neck and the first finger now plays all notes on the third fret, the second finger plays notes on the fourth fret, and so on.

power chord A guitar-specific, two-note chord that consists of a root note and a fifth. Sometimes the root note is doubled an octave higher to create a bigger sound. Since a power chord contains no third, it is neither major nor minor. The symbol "5" is used to denote a power chord (e.g. C5 = C power chord).

primary chords These are the three major chords found in any major key, and built on the first (I or tonic), fourth (IV or subdominant), and fifth (V or dominant) steps of the major scale.

pull-off A pull-off is created when only the first of two notes on the same string are picked—the second note is created by "flicking" the fretting finger slightly sideways as it is lifted off the string. If the second note is not an open string, it must be fretted throughout.

riff An ostinato (repeated) pattern, usually no more than two bars in length and often played on the lower strings of the guitar. The introduction to Smoke On The Water is probably the most famous example of a guitar riff.

scale A series of stepwise ascending (and descending) notes that follow a specific intervallic template of whole (tone) and half steps (semitones). These are generally seven notes long (i.e. the major scale), but can be shorter (i.e. the five note pentatonic), or longer (i.e. the eight note diminished scale).

slide This is achieved by picking only the first note, and then sliding the fretting finger up or down the neck to a new location. The fretting finger must maintain pressure on the fingerboard when sliding or the second note will not sound.

slur A slur is written above or below notes on the stave (as a curved line) to indicate legato phrasing. Guitar players achieve legato phrasing with the use of hammer-ons and pull-offs.

stave The stave or staff is a system of five lines used to denote pitch in conventional music notation. Specific symbols denote the length of each note or rest (silence).

syncopation The emphasis of "weak" beats to create an interesting rhythm. Weak beats occur on the second and fourth beat (in 4/4 time), or on an off-beat (i.e. occurring between the main beats).

TAB Originally used to notate lute music during the Renaissance period, this is a simplified form of notation that indicates where a note should be played on the fingerboard. It does not indicate note duration or rests (silence).

tone/semitone The basic unit of measuring the distance between two notes. A tone is equivalent to a whole step (two frets) and a semitone a half step (one fret).

three-chord trick The process of creating an entire accompaniment for a song using the three primary chords I (tonic), IV (subdominant) and V (dominant). Many popular songs are based on these three chords since they represent the principle harmonic movement in Western harmony.

Index

Key

Use this handy pull-out guide as a quick reference to the symbols and terms used in the chord and scale libraries.

Chord library

⊗ Open string not sounded in chord.

◉ Open string sounded in chord.

▣ Open string root note sounded in chord.

❶ Indicates location of the note on the fingerboard and which finger should be used to play it. The red color means this is a non-root note and so will not be the same letter name as the chord.

❶ Indicates fingerboard finger positioning (the number indicates which finger should be used) and also that the fretted note is a root note.

❶ A line crossing two or more strings denotes a barre, where two or more strings are fretted simultaneously with one finger.
❶

3 The number below the first fret of the chord box indicates which section of the guitar fingerboard the box relates to—"1" indicates first fret and higher numbers indicate the chord is played higher up the neck.

(2) ❶ Alternative fingerings are occasionally provided next to the blue and red symbols. These are sometimes preferable for a quicker change to a particular chord shape.

Scale library

❶ Indicates fingerboard finger positioning (the number indicates which finger should be used) and also that the fretted note is a root note.

❶ Indicates location of the note on the fingerboard and which finger should be used to play it. The red color means this is a non-root note and so will not be the same letter name as the chord.

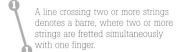 Where no finger number is given, the fingering remains unchanged and "in position."

❶ Black number indicates that the scale fingering moves "out of position."

▣ Open string sounded in chord.

◉ Open string root note sounded in chord (e.g. an E note in an E chord).

1 The number below the first fret of the scale box indicates which section of the guitar fingerboard the box relates to—"1" indicates first fret and higher numbers indicate the scale is played higher up the neck.

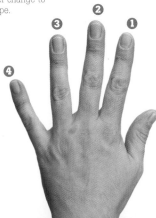

Finger numbers
Standard hand fingering has been used throughout.

Quarto would like to thank and
acknowledge the following for supplying
images reproduced in this book:

Key:
a = above, b = below, l = left, r = right

12 Marc Sharratt/Rex Features
244a, 245a, 247br KORG
244bl, 244br Wittner GmbH & Co. KG
246 Marshall Amplification plc.
247a The Epiphone Company, a part of
    the Gibson family of brands
247bl Line 6 UK, Ltd

Special thanks also to Holiday Music
for providing instruments and accessories
for photography:

Holiday Music
396-398 High Road
Leytonstone
London E10
www.holidaymusic.co.uk

All other images are the copyright of
Quarto Publishing plc. While every effort
has been made to credit contributors,
Quarto would like to apologize should
there have been any omissions or errors—
and would be pleased to make the
appropriate correction for future editions
of the book.

Credits